GREEK KEY WORDS

Greek Key Words is a learning aid benefiting from computer analysis of the surviving corpus of Classical Greek literature, comprising over 2,000,000 words. It consists of a list of the most common two thousand words in ancient Greek, with their meanings in English, arranged in decreasing order of frequency. The list is divided into a hundred units of twenty key words each, from which many more words can be derived.

Greek Key Words is the most efficient and logical way to acquire the basic vocabulary of Greek. Most grammars and readers introduce words almost at random, so that a student can never be sure of mastering commonly-occurring words within a reasonable period. A frequency list such as *Greek Key Words* can create confidence and a sense of security in vocabulary building and, by dividing the list into manageable units, mastery can be achieved without undue strain.

Greek Key Words is also weighted towards the authors who appear most often in examinations as set-texts or as the basis for unseen translation. It is therefore of the maximum possible practical benefit for those working towards public examinations.

Dr Jerry Toner has made sure that both adult beginners and school children alike will be introduced to all the most frequently-occurring words in Greek within their first year or two of study. The two thousand key words account for 85% of all word occurrences in Greek. An English index allows the reader to trace each word in the list and indicates by its position the relative frequency of that word. Dr Toner is the author of *Latin Key Words* and *Rethinking Roman History*.

D1572445

GREEK
KEY WORDS

the basic 2,000-word vocabulary
arranged by frequency in a
hundred units

with comprehensive Greek and
English indexes

JERRY TONER

The Oleander Press

The Oleander Press Ltd
16 Orchard Street
Cambridge
CB1 1JT
England

The Oleander Press
1133 Broadway, Suite 706
New York, N.Y. 10010
U.S.A.

© 2004 The Author and The Oleander Press

ISBN 0-906672-85-6

Jerry Toner has asserted his moral and other rights under the Copyright, Designs and
Patents Act, 1988 to be identified as the author of this work.

A CIP catalogue record for the book is available from the British Library.

Typeset in Great Britain and printed and bound in India

Contents

Introduction

It was when I learnt to address a cow in the vocative that I first thought there must be a better way of learning Classical Greek. Some twenty-five years later, still having failed to find an occasion to greet a bovine friend, I have designed *Greek Key Words* as an efficient, logical and practical computer-based word-list for English-speaking learners of ancient Greek in their first and second year. It is also a valuable revision tool for more advanced students.

The basic two thousand 'key' words are so called because by learning these the student acquires the basic knowledge to open up the whole world of Greek literature but also because they unlock the door to many thousands more words: plurals from singulars, feminines from masculines or neuters, and verb endings from the root.

The purpose of this technique is simply to stimulate confidence in the learning of Greek by beginning with the most common words. Nothing is more daunting to the beginner than to face the canon of obscure words that has always hitherto traditionally greeted the learner of Greek.

Greek Key Words is intended to be used with a conventional grammar and a conventional dictionary, but a massive dictionary has been found in practice to unnerve the beginner, while most available readers introduce too early words or ideas which may be arbitrary or advanced. At this sensitive phase, where interest in learning Greek can be so easily discouraged, it is suggested that the student should learn words in units of about twenty 'key' words each, thus mastering two thousand such words by the end of the first or second year. Only then will the student be able to accumulate arbitrary words of low occurrence, many of which will in any case be related to words already learnt. Computer-based methods are common to nearly all walks of life now, but statistical sampling has hitherto been rarely practised in language-learning. The Oleander Press pioneered this approach in *French Key Words* (1984) by Xavier-Yves Escande, *Italian Key Words* (1992) by Gianpaolo Intronati, *Spanish Key Words* (1993) by Pedro Casal, *German Key Words* (1994) by Dieter Zahn, *Arabic Key Words* (1994) by David Quitregard, and *Latin Key Words* (2002) by myself.

The Units
Each of the hundred units is self-contained, Unit 1 including the twenty most common key words, Unit 2 the next most common and so on. The key word is followed by an indication of its part of speech: *adj.*, adjective; *adv.*, adverb; *conj.*, conjunction; *f.*, feminine noun; *m.*, masculine noun; *n.*, neuter noun; *interj.*, interjection; *num.*, numeral; *dual*, dual; *part.*, particle; *prep.*, preposition; *pron.*, pronoun.

Many Greek words can be translated by a number of English equivalents. It would be counter-productive, in a work designed to stimulate interest rather than to clog the memory, to list all such equivalents, so only the most common have been cited.

The Indexes
The two indexes permit the reader to use *Greek Key Words* as a basic dictionary, but let it be repeated that a dictionary should be used in conjunction with this book. A concise and basic grammar should also be used. The English index is arranged in the order of the English alphabet; the Greek index is not so arranged, but in the order of the Greek alphabet.

Another fascinating usage of the indexes is to discover how frequent and useful each Greek word happens to be. Of course the frequency level applies only to the *Greek* words: nothing is implied about the relative frequency of their English equivalents. The first 10 words are so common that they account for 27% of total occurrences in a huge lexical universe; the first hundred account for 52%; and the first thousand for 75%. The full 2000 key words represent 85% of all Greek words in a corpus of over two million. It is therefore evident that anyone who masters the vocabulary in *Greek Key Words* is more than three quarters of the way to mastering the entire corpus of Greek texts.

The Sources

Greek Key Words focuses on the classical authors favoured by examination boards and universities. It includes the major works of the following authors: Aeschylus, Aristophanes, Aristotle, Callimachus, Demosthenes, Euripides, Herodotus, Hesiod, Homer, Plato, Plutarch, Sophocles, Strabo, Theocritus, Thucydides, and Xenophon. The whole of the New Testament has also been included.

Extra weighting has been given to works according to their frequency of appearance in public examinations in the UK and USA. Extra weighting has also been given to poetry so that the more common poetical words also appear in the list.

Finally, I should like to thank the Oleander Press for giving me this chance to give newcomers to the wonderful Greek language a means of not necessarily talking to cows.

Cambridge, 2003   *Jerry Toner*

Regular Verbs in
the Present Tense
(with contractions shown)

	λέγω		I say
λέγω	I say	λέγομεν	we say
λέγεις	you (s.) say	λέγετε	you (pl.) say
λέγει	he/she/it says	λέγουσι(ν)	they say

	φιλέ-ω		I love
φιλῶ	I love	φιλοῦμεν	we love
φιλεῖς	you love	φιλεῖτε	you love
φιλεῖ	he loves	φιλοῦσι(ν)	they love

	ὁρά-ω		I see
ὁρῶ	I see	ὁρῶμεν	we see
ὁρᾷς	you see	ὁρᾶτε	you see
ὁρᾷ	he sees	ὁρῶσι(ν)	they see

	δηλό-ω		I show
δηλῶ	I show	δηλοῦμεν	we show
δηλοῖς	you show	δηλοῦτε	you show
δηλοῖ	he shows	δηλοῦσι(ν)	they show

	τίθημι		I place
τίθημι	I place	τίθεμεν	we place
τίθης	you place	τίθετε	you place
τίθησι(ν)	he places	τίθεασι(ν)	they place

Unit 1

ὁ, ἡ, τό	pron.	the, that, he, she, it
καί	conj.	and, even
δέ	part.	but, on the other hand, then
εἰμί		to be
εἰς	prep. + acc.	into, to
αὐτός, αὐτή, αὐτό	pron.	self
οὗτος, αὕτη, τοῦτο	pron.	this
μέν	part.	but, on the one hand, then
τις, τι	part.	any one, any thing
τε	part.	and
τίς, τί	pron.	who? which?
γάρ	part.	for
οὐ	adv.	not
ὅς, ἥ, ὅ	pron.	this, that, who, which
πρός	prep. + acc., gen. & dat.	from, to, near
ἐπί	prep. + acc., gen. & dat.	on, upon
ἐγώ	pron.	I
ὥς	adv.	so, thus
ἐν	prep. + dat.	in
ἐκ	prep. + gen.	from, out of

Unit 2

ἀλλά	conj.	otherwise, but
σύ	pron.	you
γίγνομαι		to come into being, happen
κατά	prep. + acc. & gen.	down, downwards
ἔχω		to have, hold
ἤ	conj.	or, than
πᾶς	adj.	all
μή		not
ἄλλος	adj.	other, another
περί	prep. + gen., dat. & acc.	around
πολύς	adj.	many, much
ὑπό	prep. + gen., dat. & acc.	under, by, towards
ποιέω		to make, do
λέγω		to lay, choose, say
ἕ	pron.	himself, herself
δή	part.	indeed, in truth
ἀπό	prep. + gen.	from, away from
εἰ	conj.	if, whether
διά	prep. + gen. & acc.	through, by means of
πόλις	f.	city

Unit 3

ὅδε, ἥδε, τόδε	pron.	this
τῇ	dat. fem. of ὁ	here, there
ἀνήρ	m.	man
λόγος	m.	word, reason
ἐπεί	conj.	after, since, when
οὐδείς	adj.	no one, none, nobody
ὡς	adv.	as, how
γε	part.	at least, at any rate
φημί		to declare, say
ἐάν	conj.	if
ὅστις, ἥτις, ὅ τι	pron.	anyone who, anything which
νῦν	adv.	now
ἑαυτοῦ	pron.	of himself, absolutely
μέγας	adj.	big, great, large
τῷ	dat. neut. of τό	therefore, thereupon
ἐκεῖνος, ἐκείνη, ἐκεῖνον	pron.	that person, that thing
ἴσος	adj.	equal, like
οὖν	adv.	therefore
μετά	prep. + acc., gen. & dat.	among, after, with
ἄν	part.	would

Unit 4

παῖς	m. & f.	child
ἀνά	prep. + gen., dat. & acc.	up, upon
τοιοῦτος	adj.	such as this, so
ὅσος	adj.	as great as, how much
θεός	m.	God, god
πρότερος	adj.	before
βασιλεύς	m.	king
λαμβάνω		to take, receive
ἔτι	adv.	yet, still
καλέω		to call, summon
εἷς, μία, ἕν	adj.	one
παρά	prep. + gen., dat. & acc.	beside
δίδωμι		to give
γυνή	f.	woman
ὅτι	conj.	that
ἠμί		to say
δοκέω		to think, suppose
οὔτε	adv.	and not, neither...nor
οἷος	pron.	such as, what kind
εἶπον	aor. of ἔπω	to speak, say

Unit 5

ἔρχομαι		to come, go
δέω		to bind, tie, lack, want
δύο	num.	two
σός	adj.	thy, thine, your, yours
καλός	adj.	beautiful
εἶμι		to go
ὥστε	adv., conj.	as, as being, so as to
ναῦς	f.	ship
σφεῖς	pron.	they
ἕκαστος	adj.	every, each
ἐμός	pron.	mine
ἄνθρωπος	m.	man
μόνος	adj.	alone
δύναμις	f.	power, strength
βούλομαι		to wish, be willing
φίλος	adj.	loved, dear
μάλιστα	adv.	most, most of all
ἕτερος	adj.	the other, one of two
οὐδέ	part., adv.	but not, not even
ἄγω		to lead, carry, bring

Unit 6

κακός	adj.	bad
ὁράω		to see
φέρω		to bear
οἶδα	perf. of εἴδω	to know
μᾶλλον	adv.	more
πράσσω		to do, achieve
ἅπας	adj.	all together
χρόνος	m.	time
ἄρα	part.	then, therefore
πρῶτος	adj.	first, foremost
ἀρχή	f.	beginning, origin, power, rule
τότε	adv.	at that time, then
πόλεμος	m.	battle, fight, war
δύναμαι		to be able
φαίνω		to make appear, (pass. to appear)
πείθω		to persuade
νομός	m.	law, custom
ἅμα	prep. + dat.	at the same time as
ἀγαθός	adj.	good
ὥσπερ	adv.	just as, even as

Unit 7

ἄρχω		to begin, rule
χώρα	f.	place, country
αὐτοῦ	adv.	at the very place, just here
μηδείς, μηδεμία, μηδέν	pron.	no one, nobody
χείρ	f.	hand
ἀλλήλων	gen. pl.	one another
αἱρέω		to seize, take
ἀκούω		to hear
τυγχάνω		to hit, happen
ἐθέλω		to wish
πατήρ	m.	father
ἵστημι		to make stand
ὄνομα	n.	name
πλῆθος	n.	crowd, multitude
ἀεί	adv.	always, forever
δεῖ		it is necessary
εἶδον		to see
θάλασσα	f.	sea
πέμπω		to send
πάρειμι		to be present

Unit 8

ἐρῶ		to speak of, tell
σύν	prep. + dat.	with
ἵημι		to set in motion, send
ὑπέρ	prep. + gen. & acc.	over, above
διό	conj.	wherefore
τίθημι		to set, put, place
ἀφικνέομαι		to arrive
κελεύω		to order
ἐάω		to allow
καθίστημι		to set down, place
γένος	n.	race, family, sort, class
δείκνυμι		to show
φεύγω		to flee
ἵνα	conj.	in order to
τοσοῦτος	pron.	so large, so great, so big
βάλλω		to throw
μέσος	adj.	middle
λοιπός	adj.	remaining
χρῆμα	n.	thing, money
καθά	adv.	according as, just as

Unit 9

ὅπως	conj.	as, in such manner as, how, in order that
ὀλίγος	adj.	few, small
ἔργον	n.	work
νομίζω		to think
μηδέ	part.	but not, nor
τρόπος	m.	way, direction, manner
ἀριθμός	m.	number
συμβαίνω		to agree, happen
μέλλω		to intend to do, to be about to do
υἱός	m.	son
εὐθύς	adj., adv.	straight, immediately
πάλιν	adv.	back, backwards
ποταμός	m.	river
δίκαιος	adj.	just, civilised
εὖ	adv.	well
γιγνώσκω		to know, perceive, learn
ἵππος	m. & f.	horse, mare
μέρος	n.	part, share
πότε	part.	when, at some time
πάσχω		to suffer

Unit 10

γαῖα	f.	land, earth
οἴομαι		to think
πῶς	adv.	how?
σῶμα	n.	body
ὀρθός	adj.	straight, right
ἐνταῦθα	adv.	here, there
παρέχω		to provide, supply
πολέμιος	adj.	warlike, hostile
μέχρι	adv.	up to, so far as
πλείων	adj.	more, larger, bigger
πρᾶγμα	n.	deed, act
μήτηρ	f.	mother
σύμμαχος	adj.	ally
ἧδος	n.	delight, enjoyment, pleasure
εὑρίσκω		to find
θνήσκω		to die
ἤδη	adv.	already, now
κεῖμαι		to lie
πηρός		disabled, maimed
νικάω		to conquer

Unit 11

γῆ	f.	earth
ἔπειτα	adv.	thereupon, then
μήτε		and not, neither...nor
τεῖχος	n.	wall
πρίν	adv.	before
χράω		attack, be eager to, supply
ἔοικα		to be like, seem
τέκνον	n.	child
ὑπάρχω		to begin
ὅταν	adv.	whenever
οἰκέω		to inhabit, live in
μάχη	f.	battle, fight
ἑκάτερος	adj.	each of two, either
αὖ	adv.	again
στρατηγός	m.	general, commander
ποῦ	adv.	where
δράω		to do
δῆμος	m.	people
φύω		to bring forth, produce
ἀρετή	f.	goodness, excellence

Unit 12

ἕνεκα	prep. + gen.	on account of
κόρος	m.	boy
πολεμέω		make war, go to war
πρό	adv., prep. + gen.	before
μάχομαι		to fight
θεάομαι		to view, behold
ἔπος	n.	word
ἔτος	n.	year
ἀδελφός	m.	brother
πλέω		to sail
νύξ	f.	night
μένω		to stay, remain
ἥμερος	adj.	tame, cultivated
ἴδιος	adj.	one's own, private, personal
ἀπόλλυμι		to destroy, kill
ξένος	m.	guest, stranger, foreigner
ἀμφότερος	adj.	both
τόπος	m.	place
ἐναντίος	adj.	opposite
ἀξιόω		to think worthy of

Unit 13

μέντοι	conj.	yet, however
δεινός	adj.	terrible
ἥκω		to have come, be present
ἀνάγκη	f.	necessity
ὄρος	n.	mountain, hill
θυμός	m.	soul, spirit, heart
ἔνθα	adv.	there, then
ὅσπερ, ἥπερ, ὅπερ	pron.	the very man who, the very thing which
ἦμος	adv.	when
κρατέω		to be strong, powerful
χρή		it is necessary
πλεῖστος	adj.	most, largest, biggest
ἡγέομαι		to lead the way, guide
γωνία	f.	corner, angle
στρατιώτης	m.	soldier
ψυχή	f.	breath, life, spirit
ναός	m.	temple
χωρέω		to give way, withdraw
κοινός	adj.	common, public
πού	adv.	anywhere, somewhere

Unit 14

ἀτάρ	conj.	but, yet
ἱερός	adj.	divine, (pl.) sacrifice
βάρβαρος	adj.	barbarous, not Greek
αἴτιος	adj.	guilty
ἀληθής	adj.	true
δίκη	f.	custom, right, justice
ἡμέρα	f.	day
ἀναιρέω		to take up, raise
τέλος	n.	result, end
πολιτεία	f.	citizenship, constitution
μανθάνω		to learn
τοιόσδε, τοιάδε, τοιόνδε	pron.	such a, so great a
δῖος	adj.	godlike, divine
πολέω		to wander, plough
ὁδός	f.	road, way
πίπτω		to fall
ὕδωρ	n.	water
χέω		to pour
μέγαθος	n.	greatness, magnitude
ὅπλον	n.	weapon

Unit 15

δῆλος	adj.	clear, evident
ἀποθνήσκω		to die
κύκλος	m.	ring, circle
τετράγωνος	adj.	rectangular, square
δεύτερος	adj.	second
θυγάτηρ	f.	daughter
ἄξιος	adj.	of like value, worthy of
τιμάω		to honour
γράφω		to draw, write, (mid.) indict
πέρ	part.	though, however
κακόω		to maltreat
τελευτάω		to finish, complete
γνώμη	f.	thought, intelligence, mind
λείπω		to leave
πούς	m.	foot
χόω		to pile up
δόμος	m.	house
ῥητός	adj.	stated, specified
εἶδος	n.	form, shape, figure
σώζω		to save

Unit 16

ὅμοιος	adj.	like, similar
τρεῖς	num.	three
κομίζω		to provide, convey
ἕπομαι		to follow
ὀνομάζω		to name
κενόω		to empty
ἔθνος	n.	nation, people, tribe
ἔχις	m.	snake
ἱππεύς	m.	horseman
τιμή	f.	honour
αὖθις	adv.	back, again
μήν	m.	month
ἀδικέω		to do wrong, injure
θεά	f.	goddess
αἴρω		to take up, raise
μετρέω		to measure
ταχύς	adj.	quick, fast
κρίνω		to choose, decide
πως	adv.	in any way, somehow
τύχη	f.	luck, chance, success

Unit 17

θάνατος	m.	death
τάσσω		to arrange, marshal
βουλεύω		to deliberate, determine
δέχομαι		to take, accept, receive
πολίτης	m.	citizen
στρατεύω		to serve as a soldier
ἀφίημι		to send out, dispatch
τρέπω		to turn, direct
ἀντί	prep. + gen.	against, opposite
ζάω		to live
φράζω		to show, tell
παραδίδωμι		to transmit, surrender, betray
ὕστερος	adj.	latter, later
οὐσία	f.	being, existence
καταλείπω		to leave behind
φανερός	adj.	visible, manifest
χαίρω		to rejoice, be glad
ἀποδίδωμι		to give back, return
ὕστατος	adj.	last
χάρις	f.	grace, charm

Unit 18

ἐλάσσων	adj.	smaller, less
οἶκος	m.	house, home
δυνατός	adj.	strong, powerful
διαφέρω		to carry across, differ
κτείνω		to kill
ἀμφί	prep. + gen., dat. & acc.	around, about
πατρίς	adj.	of one's fathers
πλήν	prep. + gen.	except
τοι	part.	surely, consequently
χαλεπός	adj.	difficult
ἡδύς	adj.	sweet, pleasant
ἄριστος	adj.	best
διαφθείρω		to destroy, ruin
ἀποκτείνω		to kill
τρίγονος	adj.	triangular
ὑμός	adj.	your
ἄγαλμα	n.	delight, honour
εἴτε	interj.	would that
ὅλος	adj.	whole, complete
δηλόω		to show, reveal

Unit 19

ἀφαιρέω		to take from
βαίνω		to go
λαός	m.	people
φύσις	f.	nature
δόξα	f.	opinion, judgement
σημεῖον	n.	sign, omen
χωρίον	n.	place
κατέχω		to hold back, possess
ἀφίστημι		to remove, revolt
καιρός	m.	right time, opportunity
ἀγών	m.	assembly, contest, trial
ὧδε	adv.	in this way, so
αὐτίκα	adv.	at once, immediately
πυνθάνομαι		to learn of, hear of
τοίνυν	part.	therefore, accordingly
ἔργνυμι		to confine
παρασκευάζω		to prepare
σύμμετρος	adj.	same as, symmetrical
στάδιος	adj.	standing firm, strong
ἡγεμών	m. & f.	guide, leader

Unit 20

ὅστε, ἥτε, ὅτε	pron.	who, which
φιλέω		to love
θέα	f.	view, sight
κίνδυνος	m.	danger, risk
στάδιον	n.	stade, mile, race-course
νέω		to spin, pile
φρήν	f.	heart, mind
ἥσσων	adj.	less, worse
ἀμύνω		to keep off, ward off
ἀρχαῖος	adj.	ancient
φρονέω		to think
συμφέρω		to gather, collect, be useful
ἐμέω		to vomit
οἰκεῖος	adj.	domestic, of the home
μακρός	adj.	long, tall, deep
ἑκατόν	num.	hundred
βασιλεύω		to rule, reign
καταλαμβάνω		to seize
ἠδέ	conj.	and
τρίτος	adj.	third

Unit 21

ἔγωγε	pron.	I myself
καθό	adv.	in so far as, so that
κεφαλή	f.	head
ποῖος	pron.	of what kind?
ἑταῖρος	m. & f.	comrade, companion, prostitute
πεζός	adj.	on foot, infantry
κατασκευάζω		to equip, prepare
βάσις	f.	step, base
ἐλαύνω		to drive
παραλαμβάνω		to receive
δείδω		to fear
νέομαι		to go, come
μῆκος	n.	means, remedy
εἴκοσι	num.	twenty
πλέως	adj.	full
βίος	m.	life
νῆσος	f.	island
ὅτε	adv.	when
θύω		to sacrifice
πρέσβυς	m.	old man, elder

Unit 22

τίκτω		to bring forth, have children
οὐκέτι	adv.	no more, no longer
λανθάνω		to escape notice, forget
νέος	adj.	young
εἶτα	adv.	then, next
ἐλπίς	f.	hope
κἄν	(= καὶ ἄν)	even if, although
τρέφω		to nourish, rear
τέσσαρες	num.	four
πῦρ	n.	fire
χθών	f.	earth, ground
στρατός	m.	army
ἔπειμι		to be upon, come upon, go against
ἐφίστημι		to set up, stand over
βιόω		to live
πέντε	num.	five
ἀδύνατος	adj.	unable, powerless
ἄναξ	m.	lord, master
ἑπτά	num.	seven
κινέω		to move

Unit 23

βοηθέω		to help, aid
δέκα	num.	ten
μῦθος	m.	word, talk, story
συμφορά	f.	event, chance, mishap
ἀνδρόω		to rear up into manhood, (in pass.) reach manhood
τέμνω		to cut
αἰτέω		to ask, beg
γέρων	m.	old man, elder
πάνυ	adv.	altogether, entirely
σχεδόν	adv.	close by, almost
φόβος	m.	fear
τέχνη	f.	art, skill
πότερος	pron.	whether
βωμός	m.	platform, altar
στρατόπεδον	n.	military camp, army
παύω		to stop
μικρός	adj.	small, little
οἰκία	f.	building, house, household
φόνος	m.	murder, slaughter
πέρθω		to ravage, destroy

Unit 24

στράτευμα	n.	expedition, army
χρύσεος	adj.	golden
συνίστημι		to stand together, unite
μεταξύ	adv., prep. + gen.	between
ἀποστέλλω		to send away
ζητέω		to seek, search
τύραννος	m.	tyrant
φοβέω		to terrify
πόνος	m.	work, toil, pain
ἀναγκάζω		to force, compel
διαιρέω		to divide
ὀκτώ	num.	eight
ἐχθρός	adj.	hated, hostile
σημαίνω		to indicate, show
ὁμολογέω		to speak together, agree
ῥᾴδιος	adj.	easy
παραγίγνομαι		to be near, support
βασίλειος	adj.	royal
ὁπλίτης	m.	heavy-armed soldier, hoplite
πάθος	n.	accident, suffering

Unit 25

ἀποδείκνυμι		to point out, show
διώκω		to pursue
ὑπολαμβάνω		to take up
δόρυ	n.	tree, plank, spear
ὁρμάω		to urge, hasten
ἱκανός	adj.	sufficient
πύλη	f.	gate
σοφός	adj.	clever, wise
ἐργάζομαι		to work
τριάκοντα	num.	thirty
ἄπειμι		to be away, go away
φυλάσσω		to guard
ἄρχων	m.	ruler, chief
γοῦν	(= γε οὖν)	at any rate, any way
νέμω		to distribute, graze
ἥλιος	m.	sun
ἔξω	adv.	out, outside
πλευρόν	f.	rib, (pl.) side
ἐντεῦθεν	adv.	hence, thence
ὁπόσος	adj.	as many as

Unit 26

πολλάκις	adv.	often
ἠώς	f.	dawn
αἰσθάνομαι		to perceive
βαθύς	adj.	deep, high
προστάσσω		to place, assign
συμμαχέω		to be an ally
γάμος	m.	wedding, marriage
ἄδικος	adj.	wrong, unjust
ἡμέτερος	adj.	our
σωτηρία	f.	safety, deliverance
παρακαλέω		to call for
μιμνήσκω		to remind, (mid. & pass.) to remember
νεκρός	m.	dead body, corpse
ἀσύμμετρος	adj.	disproportionate, asymmetrical
πρᾶξις	f.	action, business
πολεμόω		to make an enemy of
ὁμόω		to unite
μετέχω		to share in
ἤν	interj.	look!
ἀπαλάσσω		to set free, release

Unit 27

πειράω		to attempt, try
μήν	part.	surely, indeed
δεῦρο	adv.	hither, to here
ἀρχήν	adv.	firstly
πορεύω		to carry, convey
ἐντός	adv., prep. + gen.	within, inside
τολμάω		to undertake, endure
περιέχω		to embrace, surround
αἰσχρός	adj.	shameful, disgraceful
κρείσσων	adj.	stronger, more powerful
ἐκβάλλω		to throw out of
ἀνάλογος	adj.	proportionate
εἰρήνη	f.	peace
προστίθημι		to put to, give, add
λίθος	m.	stone
ἦ	adv.	in truth, can it be?
αἷμα	n.	blood
ἱκνέομαι		to come
κωλύω		to hinder, prevent
πέτρα	f.	rock

Unit 28

ἄστυ	n.	city, town
χραύω		to scrape, graze
ἅπτω		to fasten, (in mid.) touch
σαφής	adj.	clear, plain
ὄλλυμι		to destroy, (in mid.) die
νόος	m.	mind, perception
βροτός	m.	mortal man
ταύτη	f. dat. οὗτος	in this way
ἄνω	adv., prep. + gen.	up, above
χράομαι		to use
βία	f.	force, power
δῶμα	n.	house, household
ἀνίστημι		to stand up, raise up
αἰτία	f.	accusation, guilt
παλαιός	adj.	old, ancient
ζέω		to boil, seethe
λύω		to loose, release
τριήρης	f.	trireme, warship
οἰκέτης	m.	house-slave
διαβαίνω		to walk, cross over

Unit 29

οὔτις, οὔτις, οὔτι	pron.	no one, nobody
δῶρον	n.	gift, present
μάλα	adv.	very, very much
ὁμοιόω		to make like
στρατία	f.	army
λιμήν	m.	harbour
ἄνω		to accomplish
ἐκεῖ	adv.	there
πιστεύω		to trust, believe in
ἐπίπεδος	adj.	at ground level
πολιορκέω		to besiege
συμμαχία	f.	alliance
ἄκρος	adj.	highest
ὅθεν	adv.	from whom, whence
ἁμαρτάνω		to miss, fail
εἴπερ	conj.	if indeed, if really
ὄντα	n. pl.	the present, reality, property
ποτός	adj.	drunk, drinkable
δοῦλος	m.	slave
ἐπαινέω		to approve, applaud

Unit 30

τελευτή	f.	completion, end
διδάσκω		to teach
πίμπλημι		to fill
ἐπιτήδειος	adj.	suitable, useful. (pl.) provisions
ἁλίσκομαι		to be caught, conquered
δεσπότης	m.	master, despot
δαίμων	m. & f.	god, goddess, genius
νόσος	f.	sickness, disease
φιλία	f.	friendship, affection
χρήσιμος	adj.	useful
θαυμάζω		to wonder, be astonished
οἴχομαι		to be gone, to have gone
ἀπέρχομαι		to go away, depart from
προσήκω		to have come, belong to
κόρη	f.	girl
ἔτης	m.	cousin, neighbour
ἀναγκαῖος	adj.	by force, compelling, necessary
ἐνδέχομαι		to accept, admit
συμβάλλω		to throw together, join

Unit 31

ἄμφω	dual	both
βλέπω		to see
δύω		to put on clothes, (aor.) take off clothes
ἡδονή	f.	delight, enjoyment, pleasure
πρόσθεν	adv., prep. + gen.	before
ὄψις	f.	appearance, sight, face
ἀπέχω		to keep off, keep away from
κώμη	f.	country town, village
εὔχομαι		to pray, vow
συνάγω		to bring together, gather, collect
ἀρόω		to plough
στερεός	adj.	stiff, firm, harsh
ἐμβάλλω		to throw in, burst in
ἡγεμονία	f.	authority, leadership
φαῦλος	adj.	easy, trivial, (of people) common
βελτίων	adj.	better
βοῦς	m. & f.	cow, bull
οὐκοῦν	adv.	therefore, then
ἐπιτρέπω		to turn towards, incline, rely on
ῥέω		to flow, gush

Unit 32

πω	part.	up to this time, yet
στόμα	n.	mouth
ἐλεύθερος	adj.	free
ἀσπίς	f.	shield
ἐμπίπτω		to fall upon, attack
παρέρχομαι		to go by, escape
θεῖος	adj.	divine, holy
συνεχής	adj.	continuous, constant
ἐκπέμπω		to send out
ὀρθόω		to set straight, set up
ἤπειρος	f.	land
τάλας	adj.	wretched
ἀμείνων	adj.	better
φυγή	f.	flight, escape
θυσία	f.	offering, sacrifice
τελέω		to complete, accomplish
τέταρτος	adj.	fourth
ἐπιτίθημι		to put on, place upon
ἐπιστήμη	f.	knowledge
σκοπέω		to look at, consider

Unit 33

πεντήκοντα	num.	fifty
ἐγγύς	adv.	near
ὄφρα	conj.	that, in order that
ἐπέρχομαι		to come upon, attack
αὖτε	adv.	again
κύριος	m.	lord, master
τάλαντον	n.	talent (a weight of money, 6,000 drachmae)
τάχος	n.	speed
ἀγορά	f.	assembly of the people, market-place
τεσσαράκοντα	num.	forty
ἐνθάδε	adv.	thither, hither, here, there
σῖτος	m.	grain, food
χωρίς	adv., prep. + gen.	separately, separate from
τρέω		to flee from
ἀναχωρέω		to go back
ἀνατίθημι		to lay upon, attribute, dedicate
πρόσω	adv.	forwards, further
ἔνιοι, ἔνιαι, ἔνια	pron.	some
δεξιός	adj.	right, lucky
τάξις	f.	arrangement, order

Unit 34

ἑκών	adj.	willing
πρόθυμος	adj.	eager, zealous
διέρχομαι		to go through
ἀναβαίνω		to go up
φυλακή	f.	watch, guard
μεταβάλλω		to change
βασιλεία	f.	kingdom
πεδίον	n.	plain
ὑπομένω		to stay behind, survive
θέω		to run
καίτοι	(= καί τοι)	and indeed, and yet
ὅπου	adv.	somewhere or other
μοῖρα	f.	part, portion, share, fate
ἐπιχειρέω		to work at, attempt
σχῆμα	n.	form, figure, appearance
ἡλικία	f.	time of life, age
μυρίος	adj.	countless, infinite
πίνω		to drink
παρίστημι		to stand, place by
ἀνδρεῖος	adj.	manly, brave

Unit 35

κτάομαι		to get, possess
νοέω		to think
θάπτω		to bury
ἔρομαι		to ask, enquire
μέγαρον	n.	hall, palace
οὐρανός	m.	heaven
ἀέκων	adj.	unwilling
ἀδελφή	f.	sister
νίκη	f.	victory
ὀξύς	adj.	sharp
ἀθάνατος	adj.	immortal, everlasting
σφόδρα	adv.	very much, exceedingly
κλύω		to hear
παρθένος	f.	virgin, girl
ἔξεστι		it is possible
καταλύω		to destroy
πονηρός	adj.	painful, bad
ἐπέχω		to have, hold from
τυραννίς	f.	tyranny
συμβουλεύω		to advise, recommend

Unit 36

ἑτοῖμος	adj.	ready, prepared
τιμωρία	f.	help, aid
στρατηγέω		to be general
εὐδαίμων	adj.	fortunate, happy
ὕψος	n.	height, top
ἀμείβω		to change, exchange
μυριάς	num. & f.	ten thousand, countless
εἰσέρχομαι		to go in, enter
ἀναλαμβάνω		to take up, assume
σφάζω		to slaughter, kill
φθάνω		to do first, do before others
συντίθημι		to put together, add
ἐρῆμος	adj.	desolate, lonely
ὀργή	f.	temperament, anger
πόσις	m.	husband
ἐνιαυτός	m.	long period of time, year
ἰσχυρός	adj.	strong
νή	part.	yes indeed
πάντη	adv.	in every way, entirely
φίλιος	adj.	friendly

Unit 37

σπονδή	f.	libation, (pl.) treaty
βλάπτω		to hinder, harm
νιν	pron.	him, her, it
χειμών	m.	winter, storm
βραχύς	adj.	short
πρόσειμι		to be present
θαρσέω		to be courageous
ἐλπίζω		to hope, expect
ὀφθαλμός	m.	eye
πολιτικός	adj.	civic, political
ἐνδίδωμι		to give in
ἀθροίζω		to gather, muster
βιάζω		to force
φάσκω		to say
ὑπόκειμαι		to lie under
ἄτε	adv.	just as, so as
ὁρμέω		to be moored, lie at anchor
δικαιόω		to think right
ὕβρις	f.	violence, arrogance
κόσμος	m.	order, ornament, world

Unit 38

ἐκλείπω		to leave out, omit
σύμπας	adj.	all together
κῆρυξ	m.	messenger, herald
ἀρχιερεύς	m.	priest
οὗ	pron.	where
εὔνοια	f.	good-will, kindness
αὐξάνω		to increase
διάνοια	f.	thought, intention
ὁπότε	adv.	when, since
γαμέω		to marry
ἱδρύω		to sit down, establish, encamp
μνήμη	f.	memory, record
ἀνάγω		to lead up, raise up
πίστις	f.	trust, faith
ἀπολείπω		to leave behind
ποιητής	m.	maker, poet
τροφή	f.	nourishment, food
πολιορκία	f.	siege
τριακόσιοι	num.	three hundred
ἡσσάομαι		to be inferior, be defeated

Unit 39

ἥμισυς adj., n. & f.	half
πάτριος adj.	of one's father, hereditary
συλλαμβάνω	to collect, gather
ἀλήθεια f.	truth
ὅμως conj.	nevertheless, still
ἦμαρ n.	day
βουλή f.	counsel, council
βλώσκω	to go, come
πλοῦτος m.	wealth
ἰσόω	to make equal
προέρχομαι	to go forward, advance
σπεύδω	to urge on, hasten
δίς adv.	twice
ἀποφαίνω	to show, display
ἥρως m.	hero
λυπέω	to distress, annoy
ὅρος m.	boundary, limit
σπουδή f.	speed, zeal
ἀσφαλής adj.	safe
ἀρετάω	to be proper, thrive

Unit 40

ἐλευθερία	f.	freedom, liberty
κοινόω		to make common, communicate
λαμπρός	adj.	bright, clear, brilliant
ὄρνυμι		to stir up
διόπερ	conj.	because of which
ἕξις	f.	possession, habit
σπουδάζω		to be keen, be busy
ἀπολύω		to undo, set free from
στρατεία	f.	expedition, campaign
προσαγορεύω		to address, greet
ᾗ	dat. f. ὅς	which way, where
εὐρύς	adj.	wide
ὑπερβάλλω		to overshoot, exceed
εἰκός	n.	likely, probable, reasonable
ἔθω		to be accustomed
ἄλλως	adv.	otherwise
κόλπος	m.	bosom
δῆτα	adv.	certainly, of course
ἅρμα	n.	chariot
ἀνέχω		to hold up, rise up

Unit 41

ὄμμα	n.	eye
χαρίζομαι		to say or do something agreeable
ἀποκρίνω		to separate, (mid.) reply
εἰκών	f.	likeness, image, portrait
κινδυνεύω		to be daring, take a risk
σφός	adj.	their, their own
πρόσειμι		to go to, approach
πόσις	f.	drink
ὁμῶς	adv.	equally, likewise
συγχωρέω		to meet, agree
στάσις	f.	standing, revolution
χρυσός	m.	gold
ἐκεῖθεν	adv.	from that place, thence
ὄρνις	m. & f.	bird
δίχα	adv., prep. + gen.	in two, apart
ἐπίσταμαι		to know
ἐπειδάν		whenever
ἐννέα	num.	nine
κυρέω		to hit, meet with
ὑψηλός	adj.	high

Unit 42

προάγω		to lead forward
δάκρυον	n.	tear
στόλος	m.	expedition, journey
ἤτοι		now surely, truly
ἐπιθυμέω		to desire
χάλκεος	adj.	made of copper, bronze or brass
παράλληλος	adj.	side by side
ῥώμη	f.	strength, might
μέτρον	n.	measure, rule
πλησίος	adj.	near, close to
κατηγορέω		to speak against, accuse
ἐκτός	adv., prep. + gen.	outside, beyond, without
χειρόω		to manage, subdue
χρηστός	adj.	useful
θεωρέω		to look at
οἰκοδομέω		to build
ἱερεύς	m.	priest
βέλος	n.	missile, arrow
ἐλάχιστος	adj.	smallest, least
φάος	n.	light, daylight

Unit 43

γράμμα	n.	letter, musical note
ἕξ	num.	six
τάφος	m.	funeral, grave
ἰσχύς	f.	strength
ἐκπίπτω		to fall out of
τεύχω		to prepare
ἐξέρχομαι		to go, come out of
διακόσιοι	num.	two hundred
ἐρωτάω		to ask
συγγενής	adj.	born with, family member
ὑπερβολή	f.	excess, superiority
ἀείδω		to sing
φίλτατος	adj.	dearest
φονέω		to make a sound
ἀπάγω		to lead away, carry off
ἄγγελος	m. & f.	messenger
ἀναγκαῖον	n.	prison, jail
τάχα	adv.	quickly
λίμνη	f.	lake
προφήτης	m.	prophet

Unit 44

ἀνάθημα	n.	curse
ναυμαχία	f.	sea-battle
ἦθος	n.	custom, character
ἀποπέμπω		to send away, dismiss
προσεῖπον		to speak to, address
αὐτόθι	adv.	on the spot
συνέρχομαι		to go together, meet
προσπίπτω		to fall upon, attack
ὑπερέχω		to hold above
ἀπορία	f.	difficulty, shortage
πυραμίς	f.	pyramid
φύλαξ	m.	guard
σώφρων	adj.	sensible, wise
αἰχμάλωτος	adj.	prisoner
ἔσχατος	adj.	furthest, extreme
σύγκειμαι		to lie together, agree
διαφεύγω		to flee through, escape
ἀνίημι		to send up, allow
ἑξήκοντα	num.	sixty
ἐνέργεια	f.	action, energy

Unit 45

δημοκρατία	f.	democracy
πληρόω		to fill up
ἥκιστος	adj.	least
φωνή	f.	voice
χρεών	n.	necessity, fate
μισθός	m.	wages, pay
προσφέρω		to bring to
ἄριστον	n.	breakfast
κάμνω		to work
δικαιοσύνη	f.	righteousness, justice
καθόλου	adv.	on the whole, in general
συνάπτω		to join together, unite
σφέτερος	adj.	their own, their
τόξον	n.	bow
πόντος	m.	sea
ὄμνυμι		to swear to
μεταπέμπω		to send after
κέρας	n.	horn, wing
ὀλιγαρχία	f.	oligarchy, rule by the few
προδίδωμι		to give beforehand, betray

Unit 46

τίνω		to pay a price
ἀκρόπολις	f.	citadel
ὁρίζω		to divide, separate from
θνητός	adj.	mortal
νομοθέτης	adj.	lawgiver
πύργος	m.	tower
γλῶσσα	f.	tongue
ξίφος	n.	sword
φυγάς	m. & f.	fugitive, exile
ἐφίημι		to send to, send against
ὅμηρος	m.	pledge, surety, hostage
κράτος	n.	strength, power
προαίρησις	f.	purpose, plan
κίνησις	f.	movement, motion
οἴκαδε	adv.	homewards
ἡνίκα	adv.	when, since
ἐκκλησία	f.	assembly, church
ἔνειμι		to be in, be possible
ἐλασσόω		to diminish
μισέω		to hate

Unit 47

μνηστήρ	m.	suitor
ἰσθμός	m.	narrow passage, isthmus
κάκη	f.	wickedness, vice
διανοέομαι		to intend, think of
τειχέω		to build walls, fortify
ὄχλος	m.	crowd, mob
κολάζω		to correct, punish
πεντακόσιοι	num.	five hundred
ἐσθλός	adj.	good
ἄνεμος	m.	wind
διαφορά	f.	difference, disagreement
προερέω		to say beforehand
ἀγωνίζομαι		to compete for a prize
πάσσω		to sprinkle
προσάγω		to bring to
ἐπιζεύγνυμι		to join, bind
καταβαίνω		to go down, come down
ἄνευ	prep. + gen.	without
σύνειμι		to be with, go with
ἀξιόλογος	adj.	noteworthy, important

Unit 48

λύπη	f.	pain
τιμωρέω		to help, avenge
μνῆμα	n.	memorial, monument
εὐδαιμονία	f.	wealth, happiness
ἀπαγγέλλω		to report, announce
καίπερ	conj.	although
ἐπάγω		to bring on, lead on
πιστός	adj.	faithful, trustworthy
ἔθος	n.	custom, habit
μηχανή	f.	instrument, machine
λόφος	m.	back of the neck, crest, mane
ἀργύριον	n.	silver coin, money
ἔργω		to shut in, enclose
ἐλευθερόω		to free
δρόμος	m.	course, running
καταστρέφω		to overturn, (mid.) subdue
ἅλς	m.	salt
θύρα	f.	door
ἀγγέλλω		to announce
διαλέγομαι		to converse, discuss

Unit 49

λευκός	adj.	bright, clear
κοσμέω		to arrange, adorn
κατοικέω		to colonise, settle
φθείρω		to ruin, destroy
μέτριος	adj.	average, moderate
κύων	m. & f.	dog, bitch
μεθίημι		to let go, release
ἔρως	m.	love
βαρβαρόομαι		to become barbarous
χείρων	adj.	worse
ἀπολαμβάνω		to take from
ἀκολουθέω		to follow
ἐμαυτοῦ	pron.	of me, of myself
μένος	n.	force, strength
κρίσις	f.	selection, decision, trial
πατρῷος	adj.	of one's father, inherited
πλοῖον	n.	ship, vessel
μέλω		to be cared for
ἀγνοέω		to not know
ὅρκος	m.	oath

Unit 50

οἴμοι	interj.	ah me! woe is me!
βέλτιστος	adj.	best
σής	m.	moth
φρουρέω		to guard
βασιλικός	adj.	royal, kingly
διαλύω		to break up, undo
κάθημαι		to sit
γόνυ	n.	knee
ὠφελέω		to help
τελευταῖος	adj.	last
ἔλεγος	m.	lament
ἐπιεικής	adj.	suitable, fair
μίγνυμι		to mix
κέντρον	n.	spur
πέμπτος	adj.	fifth
ἕως	conj., adv.	until, while
δώδεκα	num.	twelve
προσέρχομαι		to go to
ὥρα	f.	period of time
ὁμώνυμος	adj.	having the same name

Unit 51

ἐξουσία	f.	power, authority
ἑορτή	f.	feast, holiday
αἶσχος	n.	shame
ἔμπροσθεν	adv., prep. + gen.	before
χρεία	f.	use, need
περάω		to pass
βιάω		to constrain
βαρύς	adj.	heavy
ναυτικός	adj.	nautical
ἁρπάζω		to seize
διατρίβω		to rub away, waste, delay
ἄλογος	adj.	speechless, irrational
ἐξαιρέω		to take out
ὦμος	m.	shoulder
γενεά	f.	race, family
παιδεία	f.	education
μέλος	n.	limb, song, tune
ἐπιστολή	f.	message, letter
βοάω		to shout
ἕλκω		to draw, drag

Unit 52

νόμιμος	adj.	customary, lawful
κρύπτω		to hide
ὑμέτερος	adj.	your, yours
κυκλόω		to encircle, surround
πλούσιος	adj.	rich
τέλειος	adj.	finished, complete
ἀγορεύω		to speak, proclaim
ἐπείγω		to press upon, urge
ἄρσην	adj.	male
παραινέω		to exhort, advise
πύθω		to rot
ὀπίσω	adv.	backwards
κλαίω		to weep
πονέω		to labour
ἔνος	adj.	last year's
ὑβρίζω		to run riot, insult
θηράω		to hunt
πάρος	adv., prep. + gen.	before
οἴμη	f.	song
παραβάλλω		to throw to

Unit 53

ἑκούσιος	adj.	voluntary
προσλαμβάνω		to take besides
παρασκευή	f.	preparation
παντάπασι	adv.	altogether
γενναῖος	adj.	suitable to one's birth, notable, noble
γῆρας	n.	old age
ἐκδίδωμι		to give up, surrender
χίλιοι	num.	thousand
προσβάλλω		to strike against
ἐσθής	f.	clothing
καρπός	m.	fruit
πρόκειμαι		to set before
ἥδομαι		enjoy oneself
ἔρδω		to do
ὑφή	f.	web
φρουρά	f.	watch, guard
οὕνεκα	conj., prep. + gen.	on which account, because of
ἀντέχω		to hold out
γένεσις	f.	origin, creation, descent
νομοθετέω		to make laws

Unit 54

τετρακόσιοι	num.	four hundred
στῆθος	n.	breast
ἐσθίω		to eat
παρίημι		to let fall, leave out
μαίνομαι		to be furious
πέλω		to go, be
χῶρος	m.	land, country
οἰκίζω		to colonise, settle
ἀλλότριος	adj.	another's, foreign, strange
καίω		to light, burn
καταφεύγω		to flee
ἀριστερός	adj.	left, sinister
διάφορος	adj.	different
ναίω		to inhabit
κοινέω		to share in
μάντις	m.	seer, prophet
ἄκρα	f.	headland, summit
ἐπιμελέομαι		to take care of
ἐπιχώριος	adj.	rural
ἐπιδείκνυμι		to exhibit

Unit 55

εἰκάζω		to portray, liken
μάλη	f.	arm-pit, ὑπὸ μάλης = underhand
κέρδος	n.	profit, advantage
εὐτυχέω		to be successful, prosperous
ποίησις	f.	creation, poetry
χρησμός	m.	oracle
οὔπω	adv.	not yet
ὑπολείπω		to leave behind
πορθέω		to destroy
εἰσοράω		to look into
κορυφή	f.	head, top
ὄλεθρος	m.	destruction, death
γνώριμος	adj.	well-known, familiar
σοφία	f.	skill, wisdom
προθέω		to run before
περίειμι		to be around
μεταβολή	f.	change
διαβάλλω		to throw over, slander
πρέσβις	f.	age
συνοικέω		to live with

Unit 56

ἐπιφέρω		to put upon
πάντως	adv.	altogether
ἔγχος	n.	spear
ἀδικία	f.	wrongdoing, injustice
εἴρω		to say
βοή	f.	cry, shout
ἔσω	adv.	within
ἀποβαίνω		to get off
σπουδαῖος	adj.	serious
χαλκός	m.	copper
ἔδω		to eat
ῥίπτω		to throw
διότι	conj.	since, because
κατάγω		to lead down
πρόσφημι		to speak to, address
πρόειμι		to go forward
δισχίλιοι	num.	two thousand
οἴκοι	adv.	at home
πάροδος	f.	passing, passage
κτίζω		to found, establish

Unit 57

ἅλς	f.	sea
πλήσσω		to strike, hit
οὔκουν	adv.	not therefore, so not
λογίζομαι		to count, reckon
τάχιστος	adj.	quickest
δηιόω		to cut down, slay, ravage
πέλαγος	n.	sea
τοσόσδε	adj., adv.	so strong, so much
ἀλκή	f.	strength
πλόος	m.	sailing, voyage
κατατίθημι		to place, put
θέρος	n.	summer
φεῦ	interj.	oh!, alas!
πρέπω		to be clearly seen, to appear
φονεύω		to murder, kill
ὡσαύτος	adv.	in like manner, just so
εἴσειμι		to go into
ὑπακούω		to listen
κτῆμα	n.	possession
ἡσυχία	f.	rest, quiet

Unit 58

πολεμικός	adj.	warlike, military
κάλλος	n.	beauty
παραπλήσιος	adj.	nearly, approaching
λίαν	adv.	very, truly
ὁποῖος	pron.	of what kind
περισσός	adj.	extraordinary
αἰσχύνω		to disfigure, dishonour, shame
ἀποπλέω		to sail away
καταφρονέω		to look down on, despise
ἐπιφανής	adj.	evident, conspicuous
νύμφη	f.	bride, nymph
ἰός	m.	arrow
εὔνους	adj.	well-disposed, kindly
κῦμα	n.	wave
ποιός	adj.	of a certain kind
ἐπιθυμία	f.	desire, yearning, longing
ταράσσω		to stir up, confuse
τεῦχος	n.	tool, implement
λέων	m.	lion
πολλαπλάσιος	adj.	many times more

Unit 59

τλάω		to endure, undergo
ὄπισθεν	adv.	behind
ἰδιώτης	m.	private individual, layman, plebeian
νεάω		to plough up
εἰσάγω		to lead in, introduce
ἀποβάλλω		to throw off
μιμέομαι		to imitate, represent
βοήθεια	f.	help
προσδέχομαι		to accept
οὐδαμός	pron.	no one, nobody
ἄτοπος	adj.	out of place, strange
βέβαιος	adj.	firm, certain
ψεύδω		to lie, cheat
ξύλον	n.	wood
ἀθρόος	adj.	crowded together
πειράζω		to try
πεδάω		to bind, constrain
πρόνοια	f.	foresight, forethought
ἐπιβουλεύω		to plan, plot
ἐκφέρω		to carry out of

Unit 60

γεννάω	to have children
ἐπαγγέλλω	to tell, announce
ὑπισχνέομαι	to promise
τμῆμα n.	section, piece
κακία f.	badness, evil
ἐναντίον adv.	opposite, on the other hand
παραγγέλλω	to send a message
στρατοπεδεύω	to camp
φυσάω	to puff, blow
δαμάζω	to overpower
ὕπατος adj.	highest
κράτιστος adj.	strongest
σεύω	to hunt, chase
προεῖπον	to declare
ἐπίκλησις f.	surname
πλάτος n.	width, breadth
δωρεά f.	gift
πικρός adj.	sharp
φυλή f.	tribe
καθειρέω	to take down

Unit 61

ἀπαντάω		to meet
ἀξίωμα	n.	honour, reputation
θῆλυς	adj.	female
τέρπω		to delight
πλήθω		to be full of
ἐπικαλέω		to call upon
ἰδέα	f.	form, kind
ἐξελαύνω		to drive out
ὅπη	adv.	where, how
προαιρέω		to produce
κρατερός	adj.	strong
τειχίζω		to build walls, fortify
χορός	m.	dance, chorus
μήτις	pron.	so that no one, so that nothing
πρόφασις	f.	allegation, pretext
προθυμία	f.	eagerness
τοῖος	pron.	such
ἐξάγω		to lead out
προσέχω		to hold to, offer
δέος	n.	fear, awe

Unit 62

οἶος	adj.	alone
πρόγονος	m.	ancestor
πῆχυς	m.	fore-arm, cubit
ἐπιβαίνω		to go on
ὀφείλω		to owe
ὕλη	f.	forest, wood
καθαρός	adj.	clean
θεραπεύω		to serve
δικαστής	m.	judge
ἀνθρώπινος	adj.	human
ἐκτείνω		to stretch out
φροντίζω		to think, consider
αἶψα	adv.	suddenly
φοβερός	adj.	terrible, afraid
τύπτω		to beat, hit
ἔστε	conj.	until, up to
μέλας	adj.	black
μουσικός	adj.	musical
στενός	adj.	narrow
λαγχάνω		to obtain by lot or chance

Unit 63

ἀσθενής	adj.	weak
παράλιος	adj.	by the sea
πέλας	adj.	near, close
ἐπιβάλλω		to throw on
μηκέτι	adv.	no more, no longer
διασώζω		to preserve
βίαιος	adj.	violent
ἱκετεύω		to approach as a supplicant, beg
βαδίζω		to go slowly, walk
τόσος	pron.	so great, so vast
ἀρκέω		to satisfy
χρήζω		to need
ἀκριβής	adj.	accurate, precise
ταραχή	f.	trouble, confusion
παράδοξος	adj.	contrary to expectation, paradoxical
μῖσος	n.	hate, hatred
λέχος	n.	bed, marriage
σφαῖρα	f.	ball
ἀσφάλεια	f.	safety
ἑός	adj.	his, her, its

Unit 64

καταβάλλω	to throw down, overthrow
ἄλλοτε adv.	at another time
καταπλήσσω	to strike down, astound
ἑβδομήκοντα num.	seventy
ὑπέχω	to hold under, support, undergo
στέλλω	to arrange, get ready
φρόνημα n.	mind, spirit
πείρω	to pierce
ἀποχωρέω	to go away
φρούριον n.	fort, garrison
λιμός m. & f.	hunger, famine
πρόσωπον n.	face
ὀργίζω	to make angry
ἰδίω	to sweat
ὑλάω	to bark
συλλέγω	to collect, gather
μεθίστημι	to change
οἶνος m.	wine
κοινωνία f.	communion, association
προσαυδάω	to speak to

Unit 65

ἐπιμέλεια	f.	care, attention
ἱερόω		to consecrate
διατελέω		to finish, accomplish
ἄνοος	adj.	stupid
χαλκοῦς	m.	copper coin
πῆ	part.	in some way, somehow
θαυμαστός	adj.	wonderful
τηλικοῦτος	adj.	of such an age
φύς	m.	son
εἰσβάλλω		to throw into
ζῷον	n.	animal
στείχω		to walk, go
καταπλέω		to sail along
περιφέρεια	f.	periphery, circumference
ἀήρ	m. & f.	air
δύστηνος	adj.	wretched, unhappy
δεξία	f.	right hand, right
φορέω		to carry, wear
μηχανάομαι		to devise, construct
ἀρά	f.	prayer, curse

Unit 66

συντάσσω		to arrange
ἀνδριάς	m.	statue
δικάζω		to judge
σκέπτομαι		to look about, examine
κτῆσις	f.	acquisition, possession
τρισχίλιοι	num.	three thousand
δακρύω		to weep, cry
παντοῖος	adj.	of all kinds
παραχρῆμα	adv.	immediately
παιδεύω		to teach
μέτειμι		to be among
ἑξακόσιοι	num.	six hundred
τράπεζα	f.	table, bank
τηρέω		to protect, guard
ἀγός	m.	leader, chief
ἀποτομή	f.	cutting off, amputation
στασιάζω		to rebel, revolt
χῶμα	n.	mound, dam
προΐστημι		to set before
ἁρμόζω		to join

Unit 67

ἄπειρος	adj.	inexperienced
ὀγδοήκοντα	num.	eighty
ἀφανίζω		to hide
ἄνωγα		to command, order
πῆμα	n.	suffering, misery
πρόσκειμαι		to be placed on, be involved in
ἄθλιος	adj.	miserable
πληγή	f.	blow, strike
ζημία	f.	loss, damage
βασίλεια	f.	queen, princess
ἄπορος	adj.	difficult
πάλλω		to sway
διάγω		to carry over
κατέρχομαι		to descend
πόρω		to offer, give
πηγή	f.	stream
ἐξῆς	adv.	one after another, next
πόα	f.	grass, herb
φάλαγξ	f.	battle-line, phalanx
μῆτις	f.	wisdom, advice

Unit 68

ἐξευρίσκω		to find out, discover
ἄρτι	adv.	just, exactly
πορίζω		to provide, supply
ἐντυγχάνω		to meet
ἄγε	interj.	come on!, well!
ἴσως	adv.	equally
στοιχεῖον	n.	one of a row, letter of the alphabet
παροξύνω		to urge, provoke
κρέας	n.	flesh, meat
ἐπιβουλή	f.	plan, plot
ὁρμή	f.	assault, impulse
παπταίνω		to gaze, look after
τέμενος	n.	sacred precinct
ἐλλείπω		to leave behind, fall short
ὀστέον	n.	bone
ἀκτή	f.	headland, shore
ἀπορέω		to lack
στέφανος	m.	crown, garland, prize
δικαστήριον	n.	court
προέχω		to hold before, be first, excel

Unit 69

ὅμιλος	m.	crowd
στοά	f.	colonnade
ὄνειρος	m.	dream
καινός	adj.	new
διαρπάζω		to tear to pieces, plunder
ἀναστρέφω		to turn upside down, upset
ἕζομαι		to sit, set
συχνός	adj.	long, many
σπένδω		to pour
γέρας	n.	gift of honour, privilege
αἱρετός	adj.	eligible, chosen
εὐχή	f.	prayer
ὀρέγω		to reach, stretch out
ἐπανέρχομαι		to go back
ἀριθμέω		to count
τεκνόω		to have children
ἱστορία	f.	inquiry, knowledge, history
ἔξωθεν	adv.	from outside
παντελής	adj.	whole, complete
ἐγείρω		to wake up

Unit 70

διπλόος	adj.	double
ποιητός	adj.	made, created
ὑστεραῖος	adv.	on the next day
καρτερός	adj.	strong
ἄλοχος	f.	spouse
συμπίτνω		to fall together, agree
περιβάλλω		to throw round
δουλόω		to enslave
δόλος	m.	bait, trick
ἐκπλέω		to sail away
μά	part.	indeed
πηγός	adj.	compact, strong
λάθρη	adv.	secretly
δένδρον	n.	tree
οὖς	n.	ear
αὐδάω		to speak
κατασκευή	f.	preparation, equipment
περιγίγνομαι		to overcome, survive
δαίς	f.	feast
δόκησις	f.	opinion

Unit 71

ὕπνος	m.	sleep
ἀναφέρω		to carry up, lead up
ἐπιλαμβάνω		to seize, attack
μόλις	adv.	scarcely
πνεῦμα	n.	wind
δημόσιος	adj.	public
ἐπίκειμαι		to be laid upon, press upon
ἀρέσκω		to make amends
διατίθημι		to place separately, dispose of
ἱέρεια	f.	priestess
εἰσφέρω		to bring in
ὁδάω		to export, sell
ναυμαχέω		to fight a sea-battle
χρώς	m.	skin
ἀνάσσω		to rule
ἵζω		to sit, place
πάομαι		to get, acquire
λόχος	m.	ambush
ἐπιτάσσω		to command
ἱκανόω		to make sufficient, qualify

Unit 72

σκηνή	f.	tent, stage
αὐτοκράτωρ	m. & f.	one's own master
ἀπειλέω		to promise, threat
ἐμπίπρημι		to burn
γραμμή	f.	line
ἄφοδος	f.	departure, return
ἱππικός	adj.	equine
θερμός	adj.	hot, warm
ὑφίστημι		to place under
διοικέω		to manage, administer
καλύπτω		to cover
κίω		to go
διίστημι		to separate, divide
ἀμῶς	adv.	in some way or other
διαμένω		to remain
δωρέω		to give, present
μηνύω		to reveal, betray
φθέγγομαι		to speak, make a noise
ἄγριος	adj.	wild
ἀνοίγνυμι		to open

Unit 73

συνίημι	to bring together, perceive
τόλμα f.	courage
παρατάσσω	to draw up in order
ἧμαι	to sit
ἄκρον n.	summit
αἰθήρ m. & f.	sky
ἄσμενος adj.	glad
δίαιτα f.	way of living, lifestyle
ὁπότερος adj.	which of two
ἀξία f.	worth, value
ὠκύς adj.	quick, fast
ἁπλόω	to stretch out
τιτρώσκω	to wound
λογισμός m.	calculation, argument
θηρίον n.	wild animal
πολιτεύω	to be a citizen, take part in politics
τλήμων m. & f.	patient, bold
ξενόω	to treat as a guest
ὑποστρέφω	to turn back
τυραννεύω	to be a tyrant

Unit 74

δέμας	n.	body
μαστός	m.	breast
ἄρτιος	adj.	complete, suitable
ἄλγος	n.	pain
πυκνός	adj.	close, compact
ἔκκειμαι		to be cast out
νοσέω		to be sick
δουλεύω		to be a slave
ὅσιος	adj.	holy, pious
καταλέγω		to lay down
ὠφέλεια	f.	help
ἄλσος	n.	glade, grove
ἔξοδος	f.	exodus, way out, exit
ἑσπέρα	f.	evening
ἔνδον	adv.	within
διαπράσσω		to pass over, accomplish
ἐπιστέλλω		to send to, command
θαῦμα	n.	wonder
ἰατρός	m.	doctor
ἐπιγίγνομαι		to be born after

Unit 75

ἔρις	f.	strife, quarrel
ψευδής	adj.	lying, false
θοός	adj.	swift
προσδοκάω		to expect
ἀμελέω		to overlook
ῥύομαι		to rescue
ἄτη	f.	recklessness
ἐρύω		to drag
ἀναγράφω		to engrave, register
θρασύς	adj.	bold
ἰώ	interj.	oh!
διάκειμαι		to be in a certain state
ἀναλίσκω		to spend
πλήρης	adj.	full of
λήγω		to stop
συντελέω		to finish, accomplish
ἐμπειρία	f.	experience
δειλός	adj.	cowardly
κατορθόω		to set upright
ἀμφισβετέω		to dispute

Unit 76

ἐπαύω		to shout
ἀίσσω		to dart, glance
διαβολή	f.	false accusation, slander
τάγμα	n.	body of soldiers
ὑπέρκειμαι		to lie above
σῦς	m. & f.	pig, boar
γελάω		to laugh
ἔφοδος	f.	approach, attack
νεώτερος	adj.	younger, newer
κύβος	n.	cube, dice
βασίλειον	n.	palace
συστρατεύω		to serve together in the army
ἄγνυμι		to break
καθίζω		to sit, place
ἀνδρεία	f.	manliness
πόσος	adj.	how many?, how long?
κατασκάπτω		to *raze* to the ground, overthrow
πότνια	f.	mistress, queen
ἐγγράφω		to inscribe
σφάλλω		to throw down, overthrow

Unit 77

ἐράω		to love
ὑπεροχή	f.	superiority
ἡσυχάζω		to be quiet, rest
δέσποινα	f.	mistress, lady of the house
ἐπιφαίνω		to display, appear
πένθος	n.	grief, sorrow
νεόω		to renew
παρατίθημι		to place beside
σκευάζω		to prepare
αἵρεσις	f.	capture, choice
εἴκω		to yield, give way
ἐλέγχω		to disgrace, put to shame
θέατρον	n.	theatre
μνημονεύω		to remember
σιγάω		to be silent
πόλισμα	n.	city, community
φθόνος	m.	envy
γλυκύς	adj.	sweet
κερδαίνω		to gain, profit
μισθοφόρος	adj.	mercenary, hired

Unit 78

πόρος	m.	ford, ferry
ἐφάπτω		to bind
τίμιος	adj.	valued
ἴσχω		to restrain
φόρος	m.	tribute
περιπίτνω		to fall upon
ἔξειμι		to go out, come out
τραχύς	adj.	rough
ἐκεῖσε	adv.	thither, to that place
φιλόσοφος	m.	lover of wisdom, philosopher
μέμφομαι		to blame
προίημι		to send ahead
τείνω		to stretch
τραῦμα	n.	wound
θυμόω		to make angry
ἔπαινος	m.	approval, praise
φώς	m.	man
φλόξ	f.	flame
ἆθλον	n.	prize
ἐπιθυμιάω		to offer incense

Unit 79

πυρός	m.	wheat
ἐκπλήσσω		to drive out, astound
ὁμιλέω		to be in company with
ἐκφεύγω		to flee from
ἄνειμι		to go up
λευκόν	n.	white
ἀνύω		to accomplish, complete
ἀπόγονος	adj.	descended from
ὄνειδος	n.	reproach, blame
ἐλεέω		to have pity on
πρόσοδος	f.	approach
ἀείρω		to lift
κάτειμι		to go down
διάμετρος	f.	diameter
ἀριστάω		to have breakfast
ἀνόσιος	adj.	unholy
χιτών	m.	tunic
ἀποικία	f.	colony
ἀφανής	adj.	unseen
στερέω		to deprive of, rob of

Unit 80

κλίνω		to bend
ὠθέω		to push
μονόω		to leave alone, isolate
ἐπιτήδευμα	n.	pursuit, business
ἐγγίγνομαι		to be born in, be innate, happen in
παράδειγμα	n.	plan, example
ὀτρύνω		to encourage, urge
ὅμορος	adj.	bordering
ὑγίεια	f.	health
γεραιός	adj.	old
θρόνος	m.	seat, throne
τῇδε	adv.	here, thus
κλέπτω		to steal
χωρίζω		to separate, distinguish
ἀποδέχομαι		to accept
αἰαῖ	interj.	ah!
νέκυς	m.	corpse
νήπιος	adj.	young, child-like
μόγις	adv.	with difficulty, hardly
ἄρκτος	f.	bear

Unit 81

φρόνησις	f.	intention
αἰδέομαι		to be ashamed
κενός	adj.	empty
δέκατος	adj.	tenth
κρήνη	f.	well, spring, fountain
μακάριος	adj.	blessed, happy
ἰσχύω		to be strong
περίβολος	adj.	encircling
ποτή	f.	flight
διπλάσιος	adj.	double
ἱκέτης	m.	supplicant
ποικίλος	adj.	multi-coloured
μῆλον	n.	apple, (pl.) breasts, cheeks
θησαυρός	m.	treasure-house
φιλοτιμία	f.	ambitious
ἀποτρέπω		to turn away
στεφανόω		to be put round, crown
ἐξαπατάω		to deceive
ταῦρος	m.	bull
νυνί	adv.	now

Unit 82

ἐπώνυμος	adj.	given as a name
αἴσθησις	f.	perception
αὔτως	adv.	in this very manner, just as before
συγγνώμη	f.	acknowledgment, forgiveness
ἀραρίσκω		to join together
μεθό	(= μεθ'ὅ)	after that
κατοικίζω		to settle, colonise
εὐτυχής	adj.	successful, prosperous
αἰνός	adj.	dire, grim
αἴξ	m. & f.	goat
ἔφορος	m.	guardian, ruler
εὐτυχία	f.	good luck, success
ἱμάτιον	n.	cloak
σωφρονέω		to be sound of mind
ἄνισος	adj.	unequal, uneven
διέχω		to keep apart, separate
πέρα	adv.	beyond
θάλαμος	m.	room, chamber
ἱκάνω		to arrive, reach
πάλη	f.	wrestling

Unit 83

τοξότης	m.	archer
οὐδός	m.	threshold
ὀδόω		to direct
ἱστορέω		to inquire into, examine
πολυτελής	adj.	expensive
ἐπίγραμμα	n.	inscription, epigram
ἀπεργάζομαι		to finish off
ἔγκλημα	n.	accusation, complaint
ἀπόστασις	f.	defection, revolt
καθίημι		to send down, let fall
ἀγοράζω		to be in the agora
εὐνή	f.	bed
πτερόεις	adj.	feathered, winged
καταθνῄσκω		to die
ὁπλίζω		to get ready
στήλη	f.	block of stone, gravestone
φυσικός	adj.	natural
νόστος	m.	return home, journey
ἐπιλέγω		to choose, say in addition
ὁμός	adj.	same, shared

Unit 84

ἐρημία	f.	solitude, desert
ἐξεργάζομαι		to finish off
ἀποφέρω		to carry away, return
διαγιγνώσκω		to discern
μεταλαμβάνω		to share in, possess
θέμις	f.	custom
νεκρόω		to kill
ἐμπίπλημι		to fill up
ἐπινοέω		to contrive
ποιμήν	m.	shepherd
ἀπιστέω		to distrust
παίω		to strike
πορεία	f.	walking, march
θόρυβος	m.	noise, uproar
δεσμός	m.	yoke, fetter
περιίστημι		to place round
εὔπορος	adj.	easy
ἀφοράω		to look away
διατάσσω		to draw up, appoint
θείνω		to strike, wound

Unit 85

συνθήκη	f.	argument
οὐδέτερος	adj.	neither of the two
ἕβδομος	adj.	seventh
καρδία	f.	heart
εἶεν	interj.	well!
παιδίον	n.	child
θώραξ	m.	breastplate, chest
νεώς	m.	temple
πελταστής	m.	light-armed soldier
ποῖ	adv.	whither
ἄδηλος	adj.	unknown, obscure
κασίγνητος	m.	brother, cousin
νῖκος	n.	victory
κίων	m.& f.	pillar
μεσόω		to be in the middle
ἐπίκουρος	m.	ally
παραβαίνω		to go past
ἄργυρος	m.	silver, money
μήποτε	adv.	never
κῶνος	m.	pine-cone

Unit 86

κλῆρος	m.	lot, allotment, clergy
σεμνός	adj.	holy, solemn
ξένιος	adj.	belonging to a guest, foreign
ποιητικός	adj.	creative, poetical
γονεύς	m.	father
ψῆφος	f.	pebble, counter
οἰκειόω		to make one's own
εὔλογος	adj.	reasonable, sensible
ἔχθρα	f.	hatred, enmity
ἐπιστρέφω		to turn round, repent
ἐκτίνω		to pay
αἰτιάομαι		to blame
τρίπους	adj.	three-footed
ἐπιτελέω		to finish
ἀχεύω		to grieve
ἀδίκημα	n.	wrong, injustice
ἀλγέω		to suffer
φάρμακον	n.	drug
φείδομαι		to spare
τεκμήριον	n.	token, proof

Unit 87

ἀντιτάσσω	to face
ἄψ adv.	back, again
ἠπειρωτικός adj.	mainland
παραπλέω	to sail by
κύλινδρος m.	cylinder
προσβολή f.	approach, attack
ῥέζω	to do
κρατήρ m.	bowl
συμμίγνυμι	to mix together
μαλακός adj.	soft
ἄχρι adv., prep. + gen.	utterly, as far as, until
φιλοσοφία f.	love of knowledge, philosophy
κόπτω	to hit
οἴκημα n.	dwelling-place, house
ἀναγιγνώσκω	to know well, read
γυμνός adj.	naked
ζεύγνυμι	to yoke
φοιτάω	to roam
φήμη f.	omen, rumour, fame
ἀντίκειμαι	to lie opposite

Unit 88

προκαλέω		to invite, propose
ἐντέλλω		to command
προσκυνέω		to worship
μαθηματικός	adj.	mathematical
νότος	m.	south wind
πεντακισχίλιοι	num.	five thousand
ἀποτέμνω		to cut off
συλάω		to strip off
φρόνιμος	adj.	sensible, wise
προβαίνω		to advance
ὅθι	adv.	where
ἀπαμείβομαι		to reply
σῆμα	n.	sign, mark, token
ἐπιτυγχάνω		to succeed, meet with
ὑποτίθημι		to place under
βάζω		to say
ὀδύρομαι		to mourn for
βούλευμα	n.	plan
ἕδρα	f.	seat
δυναστεία	f.	power, sovereignty

Unit 89

πανδημεί	adv.	in a crowd, en masse
πυργόω		to build towers, exalt
ξενικός	adj.	strange, foreign
παράπαν	adv.	altogether
δισσός	adj.	double
στέργω		to love
ἀπατάω		to deceive
σφαγή	f.	slaughter
θήρ	m.	wild animal
προσποιέω		to pretend
κάρα	n.	head
τέθηρα		to be astonished
ὁμοῦ	adv.	together
αἰδώς	f.	shame, respect
κράς	f.	head
ἀσπάζομαι		to welcome
πλανάω		to lead astray
ἁρμονία	f.	agreement, harmony
ἁρπαγή	f.	rape, plunder
κλισία	f.	couch

Unit 90

πένης	m.	day-labourer, poor man
βάθος	n.	depth, height
πανταχόθεν	adv.	on every side, in every way
δεινόω		to make terrible, exaggerate
ἀοιδή	f.	song
οἰκήτωρ	m.	inhabitant
σκότος	m.	darkness
γόος	m.	weeping, wailing
κέλομαι		to urge on, call
προπέμπω		to send before
συγγένεια	f.	kin
ναύτης	m.	sailor
κυρόω		to confirm, determine
μέμονα		to strive, desire
σωτήρ	m.	saviour
ἀνάκειμαι		to be set up
ἐπικρατέω		to rule over
πιθανός	adj.	persuasive
εὐεργασία	f.	kindness, benefit
φθονέω		to envy

Unit 91

πρεσβεύω		to be eldest, be ambassador
μάρτυς	m. & f.	witness
πάθημα	n.	suffering
καθήκω		to come down, be proper
διέξειμι		to go out through
στρέφω		to turn
ἑστιάω		to entertain, feast
τελειόω		to complete
ψεῦδος	n.	falsehood, lie
εὐγενής	adj.	well-born, noble
γέλοιος	adj.	ridiculous
ἀπολογέομαι		to speak in defence
ναί	adv.	yes indeed
φανερόω		to make known
κείρω		to cut
τέλλω		to rise, accomplish
νύκτωρ	adv.	by night
θεράπων	m.	attendant, servant
προσίημι		to send towards, let approach
ἀγρός	m.	field, land

Unit 92

κατακτείνω		to kill
λυπηρός	adj.	painful
ἄντρον	n.	cave
ἐκβαίνω		to come out of
ἁμάρτημα	n.	failure
ζημιόω		to punish
σίδηρος	m.	iron
ἐφέζομαι		to sit on
ἐτάζω		to examine
ξόανον	n.	image, statue
δίφρος	m.	chariot
διαλαμβάνω		to seize, divide
σκῆπτρον	n.	staff, walking-stick
διακρίνω		to separate, distinguish
εἴσοδος	f.	entrance
λούω		to wash
ἀσκέω		to fashion, train
ὑποδέχομαι		to undertake
παρακελεύομαι		to order
εὐσέβεια	f.	reverence, piety

Unit 93

χειρίς	f.	glove
δάμαρ	f.	wife
κάτω	adv., prep. + gen.	down, under
αἰσθητός	adj.	perceptible
δεξιόομαι		to welcome
παιδιά	f.	game, sport
πόθεν	adv.	from where, whence
ἀίδιος	adj.	eternal, everlasting
πελάζω		to approach
κλεινός	adj.	famous
ῥήγνυμι		to break
γέλως	m.	laughter
ἀγγελία	f.	message
ἕκτος	adj.	sixth
μεστός	adj.	full
πάλαι	adv.	long ago
αἰνέω		to tell
ἆθλος	m.	contest
ψέγω		to blame
δοξάζω		to imagine, suppose

Unit 94

γαστήρ	f.	stomach
φθορά	f.	destruction
μέλαθρον	n.	ceiling, hall
ἐγκρατής	adj.	powerful
λεύσσω		to look, behold
σέβω		to worship
νεανίσκος	m.	young man
οἰκτρός	adj.	pitiable
ναυτικόν	n.	navy, fleet
κριός	m.	ram
ῥεῦμα	n.	stream
πέτομαι		to fly
μηρός	m.	thigh
εὐπορία	f.	abundance, solution
ἰχθύς	m.	fish
τρέχω		to run
ἄχος	n.	pain, distress
εὐδοκιμέω		to have a good reputation, be famous, be popular
μαντεῖον	n.	oracle
πορθμός	m.	ferry, strait

Unit 95

οὔποτε	adv.	never
ἀγανακτέω		to be angry
νεανίας	m.	young man
ἀνάβασις	f.	ascent
ὠνέομαι		to buy, bid for
αὐλή	f.	courtyard, hall
φθίω		to decay
ψιλός	adj.	bare
ἐπερωτάω		to question
κοῦφος	adj.	light, nimble
δεῖπνον	n.	dinner
κῦδος	n.	glory
ἀκοντίζω		to hurl a javelin
ἐξαίφνης	adj.	suddenly
μάκαρ	adj.	blessed, happy
μισθόω		to hire out
διαδείκνυμι		to show clearly
θρίξ	f.	hair
γηθέω		to rejoice
διάδοχος	m. & f.	successor

Unit 96

μορφή	f.	form, shape
διδάσκαλος	m. & f.	teacher
διαλείπω		to leave an interval
καταφέρω		to bring down
περιπλέω		to sail round
ὑποπτεύω		to suspect
ψύχω		to breathe, blow
στέγη	f.	roof
αὐτόθεν	adv.	from that place
ἀστός	m.	townsman
δέρκομαι		to see
ψηφίζω		to count, vote
ξανθός	adj.	yellow
στένω		to moan
πρᾶος	adj.	soft, gentle
ἐνδεής	adj.	in need of
δάκτυλος	m.	finger
ἠρεμέω		to keep quiet
λυγρός	adj.	miserable
ἀμφίπολος	adj.	busy

Unit 97

κυβερνήτης	m.	helmsman
ξύλινος	adj.	wooden
ἐξετάζω		to examine
συγγιγνώσκω		to agree with
τραγῳδία	f.	tragedy
γνωρίζω		to explain, discover
λέξις	f.	speech
σκοπός	m.	guardian, look-out
σκεῦος	n.	vessel, (pl.) equipment
ἁμαρτία	f.	failure, guilt
ἁπλόος	adj.	single, simple
αἰσχύνη	f.	shame, disgrace, dishonour
προσγίγνομαι		to be added to
λέκτρον	n.	bed
πανταχοῦ	adv.	everywhere
κέλευθος	f.	way, path
τηνικαῦτα	adv.	at that time, then
ἐφέπω		to pursue
κοῖλος	adj.	hollow
καταδύω		to sink

Unit 98

ἄγνοια	f.	ignorance
τρίς	adv.	three times, thrice
τάφρος	f.	ditch
κλέος	n.	rumour, glory
σύνοιδα		to share in knowledge, be conscious of
ὀιστός	m.	arrow
ὀρεινος	adj.	mountainous, hilly
περιλαμβάνω		to embrace, surround
θάρσος	n.	courage
εὐμενής	adj.	favourable
αὐχήν	m.	neck, throat
μαρτυρέω		to bear witness, testify
ἀπελαύνω		to drive away
πωλέω		to sell, barter
πόθος	m.	desire, yearning
βορέας	m.	north wind
μύρω		to flow
οἶκτος	m.	pity, compassion
δαπανάω		to spend
ἄπαξ	adv.	once

Unit 99

ἔμπειρος	adj.	experienced
ἄπιστος	adj.	not to be trusted
γέφυρα	f.	dyke, dam
κατηγορία	f.	accusation, charge
ἀμύμων	adj.	noble, excellent
ἐφίζω		to set upon
ἄλκιμος	adj.	strong
ἱερεῖον	n.	sacrificial victim
γυμνάσιον	n.	gymnastic school, (pl.) exercise
αἰγιαλός	m.	seashore, beach
ἀποδιδράσκω		to run away, escape
χόλος	m.	bile, anger
κομάω		to have long hair
αἰών	m. & f.	lifetime, era
πήγνυμι		to make fast, fix
ἐρημόω		to strip bare, desolate
ἄνωθεν	adv.	from above
ἧσσα	f.	defeat
συνέδριον	n.	council
τρόπαιον	n.	trophy

Unit 100

πάροιθε	prep. + gen.	before
ἀποστερέω		to rob
συγκαλέω		to convene
ἐφεξῆς	adv.	in order, one after another
φάραγξ	f.	ravine
πρεσβευτής	m.	ambassador
ἦτορ	n.	heart
ἐναλλάξ	adv.	crosswise, alternately
κάθοδος	f.	descent
ἀποστρέφω		to turn back
ἀποβλέπω		to look away from
ὀρύσσω		to dig
ὑγιής	adj.	healthy
ἄγη	f.	wonder, awe, envy
σπείρω		to sow
γειτών	m. & f.	neighbour
ὄνος	m. & f.	ass
νέφος	n.	cloud
μέλεος	adj.	idle, useless, unhappy
μανία	f.	mad passion, madness

Greek Index

ἀφοράω 84
ἀχεύω 86
ἄχος 94
ἄχρι 87
ἄψ 87

βαδίζω 63
βάζω 88
βάθος 90
βαθύς 26
βαίνω 19
βάλλω 8
βαρβαρόομαι 49
βάρβαρος 14
βαρύς 51
βασιλεία 34
βασίλεια 67
βασίλειον 76
βασίλειος 24
βασιλεύς 4
βασιλεύω 20
βασιλικός 50
βάσις 21
βέβαιος 59
βέλος 42
βέλτιστος 50
βελτίων 31
βία 28
βιάζω 37
βίαιος 63
βιάω 51
βίος 21
βιόω 22
βλάπτω 37
βλέπω 31
βλώσκω 39
βοάω 51
βοή 56
βοήθεια 59
βοηθέω 23
βορέας 98
βούλευμα 88
βουλεύω 17
βουλή 39
βούλομαι 5
βοῦς 31
βραχύς 37
βροτός 28
γαῖα 10

γαμέω 38
γάμος 26
γάρ 1
γαστήρ 94
γε 3
γειτών 100
γελάω 76
γέλοιος 91
γέλως 93
γενεά 51
γένεσις 53
γενναῖος 53
γεννάω 60
γένος 8
γέ οὖν 25
γεραιός 80
γέρας 69
γέρων 23
γέφυρα 99
γῆ 11
γηθέω 95
γῆρας 53
γίγνομαι 2
γιγνώσκω 9
γλυκύς 77
γλῶσσα 46
γνώμη 15
γνωρίζω 97
γνώριμος 55
γονεύς 86
γόνυ 50
γόος 90
γοῦν 25
γράμμα 43
γραμμή 72
γράφω 15
γυμνάσιον 99
γυμνός 87
γυνή 4
γωνία 13

δαίμων 30
δαίς 70
δάκρυον 42
δακρύω 66
δάκτυλος 96
δαμάζω 60
δάμαρ 93
δαπανάω 98
δέ 1
δεῖ 7

δείδω 21
δείκνυμι 8
δειλός 75
δεινός 13
δεινόω 90
δεῖπνον 95
δέκα 23
δέκατος 81
δέμας 74
δένδρον 70
δεξιά 65
δεξιόομαι 93
δεξιός 33
δέος 61
δέρχομαι 96
δεσμός 84
δέσποινα 77
δεσπότης 30
δεῦρο 27
δεύτερος 15
δέχομαι 17
δέω 5
δή 2
δηιόω 57
δῆλος 15
δηλόω 18
δημοκρατία 45
δῆμος 11
δημόσιος 71
δῆτα 40
διά 2
διαβαίνω 28
διαβάλλω 55
διαβολή 76
διαγιγνώσκω 84
διάγω 67
διαδείκνυμι 95
διάδοχος 95
διαιρέω 24
δίαιτα 73
διάκειμαι 75
διακόσιοι 43
διακρίνω 92
διαλαμβάνω 92
διαλέγομαι 48
διαλείπω 96
διαλύω 50
διαμένω 72
διάμετρος 79
διανοέομαι 47
διάνοια 38

103

ἐλλείπω 68
ἐλπίζω 37
ἐλπίς 22
ἐμαυτοῦ 49
ἐμβάλλω 31
ἐμέω 20
ἐμός 5
ἐμπειρία 75
ἔμπειρος 99
ἐμπίπλημι 84
ἐμπίπρημι 72
ἐμπίπτω 32
ἔμπροσθεν 51
ἐν 1
ἕν 4
ἐναλλάξ 100
ἐναντίον 60
ἐναντίος 12
ἐνδεής 96
ἐνδέχομαι 30
ἐνδίδωμι 37
ἔνδον 74
ἔνειμι 46
ἕνεκα 12
ἐνέργεια 44
ἔνθα 13
ἐνθάδε 33
ἔνια 33
ἔνιαι 33
ἐνιαυτός 36
ἔνιοι 33
ἐννέα 41
ἔνος 52
ἐνταῦθα 10
ἐντέλλω 88
ἐντεῦθεν 25
ἐντός 27
ἐντυγχάνω 68
ἕξ 43
ἐξάγω 61
ἐξαιρέω 51
ἐξαίφνης 95
ἑξακόσιοι 66
ἐξαπατάω 81
ἔξειμι 78
ἐξελαύνω 61
ἐξεργάζομαι 84
ἐξέρχομαι 43
ἔξεστι 35
ἐξετάζω 97
ἐξευρίσκω 68

ἑξήκοντα 44
ἑξῆς 67
ἕξις 40
ἔξοδος 74
ἐξουσία 51
ἔξω 25
ἔξωθεν 69
ἔοικα 11
ἑορτή 51
ἑός 63
ἐπαγγέλλω 60
ἐπάγω 48
ἐπαινέω 29
ἔπαινος 78
ἐπανέρχομαι 69
ἐπαύω 76
ἐπεί 3
ἐπείγω 52
ἐπειδάν 41
ἔπειμι 22
ἔπειτα 11
ἐπεροτάω 95
ἐπέρχομαι 33
ἐπέχω 35
ἐπί 1
ἐπιβαίνω 62
ἐπιβάλλω 63
ἐπιβουλεύω 59
ἐπιβουλή 68
ἐπιγίγνομαι 74
ἐπίγραμμα 83
ἐπιδείκνυμι 54
ἐπιεικής 50
ἐπιζεύγνυμι 47
ἐπιθυμέω 42
ἐπιθυμία 58
ἐπιθυμιάω 78
ἐπικαλέω 61
ἐπίκειμαι 71
ἐπίκλησις 60
ἐπίκουρος 85
ἐπικρατέω 90
ἐπιλαμβάνω 71
ἐπιλέγω 83
ἐπιμέλεια 65
ἐπιμελέομαι 54
ἐπινοέω 84
ἐπίπεδος 29
ἐπίσταμαι 41
ἐπιστέλλω 74
ἐπιστήμη 32

ἐπιστολή 51
ἐπιστρέφω 86
ἐπιτάσσω 71
ἐπιτελέω 86
ἐπιτήδειος 30
ἐπιτήδευμα 80
ἐπιτίθημι 32
ἐπιτρέπω 31
ἐπιτυγχάνω 88
ἐπιφαίνω 77
ἐπιφανής 58
ἐπιφέρω 56
ἐπιχειρέω 34
ἐπιχώριος 54
ἕπομαι 16
ἔπος 12
ἑπτά 22
ἐπώνυμος 82
ἐράω 77
ἐργάζομαι 25
ἔργνυμι 19
ἔργον 9
ἔργω 48
ἔρδω 53
ἐρημία 84
ἔρημος 36
ἐρημόω 99
ἔρις 75
ἔρομαι 35
ἐρύω 75
ἔρχομαι 5
ἐρῶ 8
ἔρως 49
ἐρωτάω 43
ἐσθής 53
ἐσθίω 54
ἐσθλός 47
ἑσπέρα 74
ἔστε 62
ἑστιάω 91
ἔσχατος 44
ἔσω 56
ἐτάζω 92
ἑταῖρος 21
ἕτερος 5
ἔτης 30
ἔτι 4
ἕτοιμος 36
ἔτος 12
εὖ 9
εὐγενής 91

105

106

ναῦς 5
ναύτης 90
ναυτικόν 94
ναυτικός 51
νεανίας 95
νεανίσκος 94
νεάω 59
νεκρός 26
νεκρόω 84
νέκυς 80
νέμω 25
νέομαι 21
νέος 22
νεόω 77
νέφος 100
νέω 20
νεώς 85
νεώτερος 76
νή 36
νήπιος 80
νῆσος 21
νικάω 10
νίκη 35
νῖκος 85
νιν 37
νοέω 35
νομίζω 9
νόμιμος 52
νομοθετέω 53
νομοθέτης 46
νομός 6
νόος 28
νοσέω 74
νόσος 30
νόστος 83
νότος 88
νύκτωρ 91
νύμφη 58
νῦν 3
νυνί 81
νύξ 12

ξανθός 96
ξενικός 89
ξένιος 86
ξένος 12
ξενόω 73
ξίφος 46
ξόανον 92

ξύλινος 97
ξύλον 59

ὁ 1
ὅ 1
ὅ τι 3
ὀγδοήκοντα 67
ὀδάω 71
ὅδε 3
ὁδός 14
ὁδόω 83
ὀδύρομαι 88
ὅθεν 29
ὅθι 88
οἶδα 6
οἴκαδε 46
οἰκεῖος 20
οἰκειόω 86
οἰκέτης 28
οἰκέω 11
οἴκημα 87
οἰκήτωρ 90
οἰκία 23
οἰκίζω 54
οἰκοδομέω 42
οἴκοι 56
οἶκος 18
οἶκτος 98
οἰκτρός 94
οἴμη 52
οἴμοι 50
οἶνος 64
οἴομαι 10
οἶος 62
οἷος 4
ὀιστός 98
οἴχομαι 30
ὀκτώ 24
ὄλεθρος 55
ὀλιγαρχία 45
ὀλίγος 9
ὄλλυμι 28
ὅλος 18
ὅμηρος 46
ὁμιλέω 79
ὅμιλος 69
ὄμμα 41
ὄμνυμι 45
ὅμοιος 16

ὁμοιόω 29
ὁμολογέω 24
ὅμορος 80
ὁμός 83
ὁμοῦ 89
ὁμόω 26
ὁμώνυμος 50
ὁμῶς 41
ὅμως 39
ὄνειδος 79
ὄνειρος 69
ὄνομα 7
ὀνομάζω 16
ὄνος 100
ὄντα 29
ὀξύς 35
ὅπερ 13
ὅπη 61
ὄπισθεν 59
ὀπίσω 52
ὁπλίζω 83
ὁπλίτης 24
ὅπλον 14
ὁποῖος 58
ὁπόσος 25
ὁπότε 38
ὁπότερος 73
ὅπου 34
ὅπως 9
ὁράω 6
ὀργή 36
ὀργίζω 64
ὀρέγω 69
ὀρεινος 98
ὀρθός 10
ὀρθόω 32
ὁρίζω 46
ὅρκος 49
ὁρμάω 25
ὁρμέω 37
ὁρμή 68
ὄρνις 41
ὄρνυμι 40
ὄρος 13
ὅρος 39
ὀρύσσω 100
ὅς 1
ὅσιος 74
ὅσος 4
ὅσπερ 13
ὅστε 20

109

ὀστέον 68
ὅστις 3
ὅταν 11
ὅτε 20, 21
ὅτι 4
ὀτρύνω 80
οὐ 1
οὖ 38
οὐδαμός 59
οὐδέ 5
οὐδείς 3
οὐδέτερος 85
οὐδός 83
οὐκέτι 22
οὐκοῖν 31
οὔκουν 57
οὖν 3
οὔνεκα 53
οὔποτε 95
οὔπω 55
οὐρανός 35
οὕς 70
οὐσία 17
οὔτε 4
οὔτι 29
οὔτις 29
οὗτος 1
ὀφείλω 62
ὀφθαλμός 37
ὄφρα 33
ὄχλος 47
ὄψις 31

πάθημα 91
πάθος 24
παιδεία 51
παιδεύω 66
παιδιά 93
παιδίον 85
παῖς 4
παίω 84
πάλαι 93
παλαιός 28
πάλη 82
πάλιν 9
πάλλω 67
πανδημεί 89
παντάπασι 53
πανταχόθεν 90

πανταχοῦ 97
παντελής 69
πάντῃ 36
παντοῖος 66
πάντως 56
πάνυ 23
πάομαι 71
παπταίνω 68
παρά 4
παραβαίνω 85
παραβάλλω 52
παραγγέλλω 60
παραγίγνομαι 24
παράδειγμα 80
παραδίδωμι 17
παράδοξος 63
παραινέω 52
παρακαλέω 26
παρακελεύομαι 92
παραλαμβάνω 21
παράλιος 63
παράλληλος 42
παράπαν 89
παραπλέω 87
παραπλήσιος 58
παρασκευάζω 19
παρασκευή 53
παρατάσσω 73
παρατίθημι 77
παραχρῆμα 66
πάρειμι 7
παρέρχομαι 32
παρέχω 10
παρθένος 35
παρίημι 54
παρίστημι 34
πάροδος 56
πάροιθε 100
παροξύνω 68
πάρος 52
πᾶς 2
πάσσω 47
πάσχω 9
πατήρ 7
πάτριος 39
πατρίς 18
πατρῷος 49
παύω 23
πεδάω 59
πεδίον 34
πεζός 21

πείθω 6
πειράζω 59
πειράω 27
πείρω 64
πέλαγος 57
πελάζω 93
πέλας 63
πελταστής 85
πέλω 54
πέμπτος 50
πέμπω 7
πένης 90
πένθος 77
πεντακισχίλιοι 88
πεντακόσιοι 47
πέντε 22
πεντήκοντα 33
πέρ 15
πέρα 82
περάω 51
πέρθω 23
περί 2
περιβάλλω 70
περίβολος 81
περιγίγνομαι 70
περίειμι 55
περιέχω 27
περιίστημι 84
περιλαμβάνω 98
περιπίπτω 78
περιπλέω 96
περισσός 58
περιφέρεια 65
πέτομαι 94
πέτρα 27
πῇ 65
πηγή 67
πήγνυμι 99
πηγός 70
πῆμα 67
πηρός 10
πῆχυς 62
πιθανός 90
πικρός 60
πίμπλημι 30
πίνω 34
πίπτω 14
πιστεύω 29
πίστις 38
πιστός 48
πλανάω 89

113

English Index

116

117

118

119

flee 8, 54
flee from 33, 79
flee through 44
flesh 68
fleet 94
flight 32, 81
flow 31, 98
fly 94
follow 16, 49
food 33, 38
foot 15
foot, on 21
for 1
force 24, 28, 37, 49
force, by 30
ford 78
fore-arm 62
foreign 54, 86, 89
foreigner 12
foremost 6
foresight 59
forest 62
forethought 59
forever 7
forget 22
forgiveness 82
form 15, 34, 61, 96
fort 64
forth, bring 11, 22
fortify 47, 61
fortunate 36
forty 33
forwards 33
found 56
fountain 81
four 22
four hundred 54
fourth 32
free 32, 48
freedom 40
friendly 36
friendship 30
from 1, 1, 2
from above 99
from outside 69
from that place 41, 96
from where 93
from whom 29
fruit 53
fugitive 46

full 21, 93
full of 75
full of, be 61
funeral 43
furious, be 54
further 33
furthest 44

gain 77
game 93
garland 68
garrison 64
gate 25
gather 20, 31, 37, 39, 64
gaze 68
general 11
general, be 36
genius 30
gentle 96
get 35, 71
get off 56
get ready 64, 83
gift 29, 60
gift of honour 69
girl 30, 35
give 4, 27, 67, 72
give back 17
give beforehand 45
give in 37
give up 53
give way 13, 77
given as a name 82
glad 73
glad, be 17
glade 74
glance 76
glory 95, 98
glove 93
go 5, 5, 19, 21, 39, 43, 54,
   65, 72
go against 22
go away 25, 30, 64
go back 33, 69
go by 32
go down 47, 79
go forward 39, 56
go in 36
go into 57

go on 62
go out 78
go out through 91
go past 85
go slowly 63
go through 34
go to 41, 50
go to war 12
go together 44
go up 34, 79
go with 47
goat 82
god 4, 30
God 4
goddess 16, 30
godlike 14
gold 41
golden 24
gone, be 30
good 6, 47
good luck 82
goodness 11
good-will 38
grace 17
grain 33
grass 67
grave 43
gravestone 83
graze 25, 28
great 3
great as, as 4
greatness 14
Greek, not 14
greet 40
grief 77
grieve 86
grim 82
ground 22
ground level, at 29
grove 74
guard 25, 34, 44, 50, 53, 66
guardian 82, 97
guest 12
guest, belonging to a 86
guest, treat as a 73
guide 13, 19
guilt 28, 97
guilty 14
gush 31
gymnastic school 99

habit 40, 48
hair 95
hair, have long 99
half 39
hall 35, 94, 95
hand 7
happen 2, 7, 9
happen in 80
happiness 48
happy 36, 81, 95
harbour 29
hardly 80
harm 37
harmony 89
harsh 31
hasten 25, 39
hate 46, 63
hated 24
hatred 63, 86
have 2, 35
have come 13, 30
have gone 30
have pity on 79
he 1
head 21, 55, 89, 89
headland 54, 68
health 80
healthy 100
hear 7, 35
hear of 19
heart 13, 20, 85, 100
heaven 35
heavy 51
heavy-armed soldier 24
height 36, 90
helmsman 97
help 23, 36, 48, 50, 59, 74
hence 25
her 37, 63
herald 38
herb 67
here 3, 10, 33, 80
hereditary 39
hero 39
herself 2
hide 52, 67, 41
high 26
highest 29, 60
hill 13
hilly 98

him 37
himself 2
himself, of 3
hinder 27, 37
hire out 95
hired 77
his 63
history 69
hit 7, 41, 57, 62, 87
hither 27, 33
hold 2
hold above 44
hold back 19
hold before 68
hold from 35
hold out 53
hold to 61
hold under 64
hold up 40
holiday 51
hollow 97
holy 32, 74, 86
home 18
home, at 56
home, of the 20
homewards 46
honour 15, 16, 18, 61
hope 22, 37
hoplite 24
horn 45
horse 9
horseman 16
hostage 46
hostile 10, 24
hot 72
house 15, 18, 23, 28, 87
household 23, 28
house-slave 28
how 3, 9, 10, 61
how long 76
how many 76
how much 4
however 13, 15
human 62
hundred 20
hunger 64
hunt 52, 60
hurl a javelin 95
husband 36

I 1
I myself 21
idle 100
if 2, 3
if indeed 29
if really 29
ignorance 98
image 41, 92
imagine 93
imitate 59
immediately 9, 19, 66
immortal 35
implement 58
important 47
impulse 68
in 1
incense, offer 78
in any way 16
in every way 36, 90
in general 45
in like manner 57
in need of 96
in order 100
in order that 9, 33
in order to 8
in so far as 21
in some way 65
in some way or other 72
in such manner as 9
in this very manner 82
in this way 19, 28
in truth 27
in two 41
in, be 46
incline 31
increase 38
indeed 2, 27, 70
indicate 24
indict 15
inexperienced 67
infantry 21
inferior, be 38
infinite 34
inhabit 11, 54
inhabitant 90
inherited 49
injure 16
injustice 56, 86
innate, be 80
inquire into 83

inquiry 69
inscribe 76
inscription 83
inside 27
instrument 48
insult 52
intelligence 15
intend 47
intend to do 9
intention 38, 81
into 1
introduce 59
invite 88
involved in, be 67
iron 92
irrational 51
island 21
isolate 80
isthmus 47
it 1, 37
its 63

jail 43
javelin, hurl a 95
join 30, 47, 66
join together 45, 82
journey 42, 83
judge 62, 66
judgement 19
just 9, 68
just as 6, 8, 37
just as before 82
just here 7
just so 57
justice 14, 45

keen, be 40
keep apart 82
keep away from 31
keep off 20, 31
keep quiet 96
kill 12, 18, 18, 36, 57, 84, 92
kin 90
kind 61
kind, of a certain 58

kind, of what 21, 58
kindly 58
kindness 38, 90
king 4
kingdom 34
kingly 50
knee 50
know 6, 9, 41
know, not 49
know well 87
knowledge 32, 69
known, make 91

labour 52
lack 5, 68
lady of the house 77
laid upon, be 71
lake 43
lament 50
land 10, 32, 54, 91
large 3
larger 10
largest 13
last 17, 50
last year's 52
later 17
latter 17
laugh 76
laughter 93
law 6
lawful 52
lawgiver 46
laws, make 53
lay 2
lay down 74
lay upon 33
layman 59
lead 5
lead astray 89
lead away 43
lead down 56
lead forward 42
lead in 59
lead on 48
lead out 61
lead the way 13
lead up 38, 71
leader 19, 66

leadership 31
learn 9, 14
learn of 19
least 42, 45
leave 15
leave alone 80
leave an interval 96
leave behind 17, 38, 55, 68
leave out 38, 54
left 54
less 18, 20
let approach 91
let fall 54, 83
let go 49
letter 43, 51
letter of the alphabet 68
libation 37
liberty 40
lie 10, 59, 91
lie above 76
lie at anchor 37
lie opposite 87
lie together 44
lie under 37
life 13, 21
lifestyle 73
lifetime 99
lift 79
light 42, 54, 95
light-armed soldier 85
like 3, 16
like, be 11
like, make 29
likely 40
liken 55
likeness 41
likewise 41
limb 51
limit 39
line 72
lion 58
listen 57
little 23
live 17, 22
live in 11
live with 55
lonely 36
long 20, 69
long ago 93
long period of time 36

shape 15, 96
share 9, 34
share in 26, 54, 84
share in knowledge 98
shared 83
sharp 35, 60
she 1
shepherd 84
shield 32
ship 5, 49
shore 68
short 37
short, fall 68
shortage 44
shoulder 51
shout 51, 56, 76
show 8, 17, 18, 24, 25, 39
show clearly 95
shut in 48
sick, be 74
sickness 30
side 25
side by side 42
siege 38
sight 20, 31
sign 19, 88
silent, be 77
silver 85
silver coin 48
similar 16
simple 97
since 3, 38, 46, 56
sing 43
single 97
sinister 54
sink 97
sister 35
sit 50, 69, 71, 73, 76
sit down 38
sit on 92
six 43
six hundred 66
sixth 93
sixty 44
skill 23, 55
skin 71
sky 73
slander 55, 76
slaughter 23, 36, 89
slave 29

slave, be a 74
slay 57
sleep 71
small 9, 23
smaller 18
smallest 42
snake 16
so 1, 4, 19
so as 37
so as to 5
so big 8
so far as 10
so great 8, 63
so great a 14
so large 8
so much 57
so not 57
so strong 57
so that 21
so that no one 61
so that nothing 61
so vast 63
soft 87, 96
soldier 13
soldier, serve as a 17
soldiers, body of 76
solemn 86
solitude 84
solution 94
some 33
somehow 16, 65
somewhere 13
somewhere or other 34
son 9, 65
song 51, 52, 90
sorrow 77
sort 8
soul 13
sound, make a 43
sound of mind, be 82
south wind 88
sovereignty 88
sow 100
spare 86
speak 4, 52, 70, 72
speak against 42
speak in defence 91
speak of 8
speak to 44, 56, 64
speak together 24

spear 25, 56
specified 15
speech 97
speechless 51
speed 33, 39
spend 75, 98
spin 20
spirit 13, 13, 64
sport 93
spouse 70
spring 81
sprinkle 47
spur 50
square 15
stade 20
staff 92
stage 72
stand 34
stand, make 7
stand over 22
stand together 24
stand up 28
standing 41
standing firm 19
stated 15
statue 66, 92
stay 12
stay behind 34
steal 80
step 21
stiff 31
still 4, 39
stir up 40, 58
stomach 94
stone 27
stone, block of 83
stop 23, 75
storm 37
story 23
straight 9, 10
strait 94
strange 54, 59, 89
stranger 12
stream 67, 94
strength 5, 42, 43, 46, 49,
    57
stretch 78
stretch out 62, 69, 73
strife 75
strike 57, 67, 84, 84

127

time of life 34
to 1, 1
to, bring 45, 47
to here 27
to that place 78
together 89
together, bring 31, 73
together, fall 70
toil 24
token 86, 88
tongue 46
tool 58
top 36, 55
touch 28
towards 2
tower 46
towers, build 89
town 28
town, country 31
townsman 96
tragedy 97
train 92
transmit 17
treasure-house 81
treaty 37
tree 25, 70
trial 19, 49
triangular 18
tribe 16, 60
tribute 78
trick 70
trireme 28
trivial 31
trophy 99
trouble 63
true 14
truly 42, 58
trust 29, 38
trusted, not to be 99
trustworthy 48
truth 39
truth, in 2
try 27, 59
tune 51
tunic 79
turn 17, 91
turn away 81
turn back 73, 100
turn round 86
turn towards 31

turn upside down 69
twelve 50
twenty 21
twice 39
two 5
two hundred 43
two thousand 56
tyranny 35
tyrant 24
tyrant, be a 73

unable 22
under 2, 93
undergo 59, 64
underhand 55
undertake 27, 92
undo 40, 50
unequal 82
uneven 82
unhappy 65, 100
unholy 79
unite 24, 26, 45
unjust 26
unknown 85
unseen 79
until 50, 62, 87
unwilling 35
up 4, 28
up to 10, 62
up to this time 32
upon 1, 4
upon, be 22
upon, fall 32, 44, 78
uproar 84
upset 69
urge 25, 52, 68, 80
urge on 39, 90
use 28, 51
useful 30, 30, 42
useful, be 20
useless 100
utterly 87

value 73
value, of like 15
valued 78

very 29, 58
very much 29, 35
vessel 49, 97
vice 47
victory 35, 85
view 12, 20
village 31
violence 37
violent 63
virgin 35
visible 17
voice 45
voluntary 53
vomit 20
vote 96
vow 31
voyage 57

wages 45
wailing 90
wake up 69
walk 28, 63, 65
walking 84
walking-stick 92
wall 11
walls, build, 47, 61
wander 14
want 5
war 6
war, make 12
ward off 20
warlike 10, 58
warm 72
warship 28
wash 92
waste 51
watch 34, 53
water 14
wave 58
way 9, 14, 97
way of living 73
way out 74
weak 63
wealth 39, 48
weapon 14
wear 65
web 53
wedding 26

weep 52, 66
weeping 90
welcome 89, 93
well 9, 68, 81, 85
well-born 91
well-disposed 58
well-known 55
what kind 4
wheat 79
when 3, 9, 21, 38, 46
whence 29, 93
whenever 11, 41
where 11, 38, 40, 61, 88
wherefore 8
whether 2, 23
which 1, 1, 20
which of two 73
which way 40
while 50
white 79
whither 85
who 1, 1, 20
whole 18, 69
wickedness 47
wide 40
width 60
wife 93
wild 72
wild animal 73, 89
willing 34
willing, be 5

wind 47, 71
wind, south 88
wine 64
wing 45
winged 83
winter 37
wisdom 55, 67
wise 25, 44, 88
wish 5, 7
with 3, 8
with, be 47
withdraw 13
within 27, 56, 74
without 42, 47
witness 91
witness, bear 98
woe is me! 50
woman 4
wonder 30, 74, 100
wonderful 65
wood 59, 62
wooden 97
word 3, 12, 23
work 9, 24, 25, 45
work at 34
world 37
worse 20, 49
worship 88, 94
worth 73
worthy of 15
would 3

would that 18
wound 73, 78, 84
wrestling 82
wretched 32, 65
write 15
wrong 26, 86
wrong, do 16
wrongdoing 56

year 12, 36
yearning 58, 98
yellow 96
yes indeed 36, 91
yet 4, 13, 14, 32
yield 77
yoke 84, 87
you 2
young 22, 80
young man 94, 95
younger 76
your 5, 18, 52
yours 5, 52

zeal 39
zealous 34

BOOKS FROM OLEANDER

THE ORESTEIA
Aeschylus, adapted by William Whallon

LATIN KEY WORDS
Jerry Toner

RETHINKING ROMAN HISTORY
Jerry Toner

CAMBRIDGESHIRE: A HISTORY OF CHURCH & PARISH
Norman Pounds

NORTH FROM GRANADA
Roy Nash

HOME IN ANDALUSIA
Roy Nash

THE COMFORT OF WOMEN: A NOVEL
Philip Ward

HIS ENAMEL MUG: NEW POEMS
Philip Ward

THE 64 SEASONS: POEMS
James Russell

WITH MY OWN WINGS: MEMOIRS
Raymond Lister

CHINGLISH
Henry Hao

JAPLISH
Yap Yarn

CONTEMPORARY DESIGNER BOOKBINDERS
Philip Ward

COASTAL FEATURES OF ENGLAND AND WALES
Alfred Steers

NATIONAL SERVICE 1950s
John Kelly

ALBANIA: A TRAVEL GUIDE
Philip Ward

BANGKOK: A TRAVEL GUIDE
Philip Ward

BEFRIENDING: A SOCIOLOGICAL CASE-HISTORY
M. Hagard & V. Blickem

BOOKS FROM OLEANDER

A LIFETIME'S READING
Philip Ward

CONTEMPORARY GERMAN POETRY: AN ANTHOLOGY
Trans. by Ewald Osers

THE NEW MAHJONG
David Pritchard

INDIAN MANSIONS: A SOCIAL HISTORY OF THE HAVELI
Sarah Tillotson

THE HIDDEN MUSIC: SELECTED POEMS
Östen Sjöstrand

BULGARIAN VOICES: LETTING THE PEOPLE SPEAK
Philip Ward

BULGARIA: A TRAVEL GUIDE
Philip Ward

SOFIA: PORTRAIT OF A CITY
Philip Ward

GREGUERIAS: THE WIT AND WISDOM OF
Ramón Gómez de la Serna

LOST SONGS: POEMS
Philip Ward

SWANSONGS: POEMS
Sue Lenier

RAIN FOLLOWING: NEW POEMS
Sue Lenier

RAJASTHAN, AGRA, DELHI: A TRAVEL GUIDE
Philip Ward

SOUTH INDIA: A TRAVEL GUIDE
Philip Ward

WESTERN INDIA: A TRAVEL GUIDE
Philip Ward

GUJARAT, DAMAN, DIU: A TRAVEL GUIDE
Philip Ward

FATHER GANDER'S NURSERY RHYMES
Per Gander

SUDAN TALES: REMINISCENCES OF BRITISH WIVES
Rosemary Kenrick

BOOKS FROM OLEANDER

A VOYAGE TO ARABIA FELIX (1708–10)
Jean de La Roque

SOUTH ARABIA ('Palinurus' Journals, 1832–6)
Jessop Hulton

RED WOLVES OF YEMEN
Vitaly Naumkin

TRAVELS IN OMAN
Philip Ward

HISTORY OF SEYD SAID
Vincenzo Maurizi

OMANI PROVERBS
A.S.G. Jayakar

MINISTER IN OMAN
Neil Innes

ANNALS OF OMAN
Sirhan ibn Sirhan

SOJOURN WITH THE GRAND SHARIF OF MAKKAH (1854)
Charles Didier

BAHRAIN: A TRAVEL GUIDE
Philip Ward

A DOCTOR IN SAUDI ARABIA
G.E. Moloney

ARABIAN GULF INTELLIGENCE (1856)
comp. R.H. Thomas

HA'IL: OASIS CITY OF SAUDI ARABIA
Philip Ward

ARABIAN PERSONALITIES OF THE EARLY 20th CENTURY
introd. R.L. Bidwell

THE GOLD-MINES OF MIDIAN
Richard Burton

TRAVELS IN ARABIA (1845 & 1848)
Yrjö Aukusti Wallin

KING HUSAIN AND THE KINGDOM OF HEJAZ
Randall Baker

REPORT ON A JOURNEY TO RIYADH (1865)
Lewis Pelly

BOOKS FROM OLEANDER

A DICTIONARY OF COMMON FALLACIES
Philip Ward

ROMAGNOL: LANGUAGE AND LITERATURE
D.B. Gregor

FRIULAN: LANGUAGE AND LITERATURE
D.B. Gregor

CELTIC: A COMPARATIVE STUDY
D.B. Gregor

FORGOTTEN GAMES: A NOVEL OF THE SPANISH CONQUEST OF MEXICO
Philip Ward

A LIZARD AND OTHER DISTRACTIONS: STORIES
Philip Ward

A MALTESE BOYHOOD: STORIES
Philip Ward

MARVELL'S ALLEGORICAL POETRY
Bruce King

DE VERE IS SHAKESPEARE
Dennis Baron

IMPOSTORS AND THEIR IMITATORS: POEMS
Philip Ward

LIBYAN MAMMALS
Ernst Hufnagl

TRIPOLI: PORTRAIT OF A CITY
Philip Ward

THE AEOLIAN ISLANDS
Philip Ward

WIGHT MAGIC
Philip Ward

FINNISH CITIES: HELSINKI, TURKU and TAMPERE
Philip Ward

POLISH CITIES: CRACOW, GDAŃSK and WARSAW
Philip Ward

JAPANESE CAPITALS: NARA, KYOTO and TOKYO
Philip Ward

LATIN KEY WORDS
Jerry Toner

The 2,000 commonest words in the Latin language are set out in
frequency order, with indexes in Latin and English, for school, college
or home use.

FRENCH KEY WORDS
Xavier-Yves Escande

A logical approach to learning the French language, listing the most
common two thousand words in order of frequency, enabling the student
to acquire a basic vocabulary in the shortest possible time.

GERMAN KEY WORDS
Dieter Zahn

By learning two thousand common words and their derivatives, the
student may quickly acquire a vocabulary of up to ten thousand words.

ITALIAN KEY WORDS
Gianpaolo Intronati

Setting the most frequently-used words in Italian in their order of
occurrence, the student will absorb up to ten thousand.

SPANISH KEY WORDS
Pedro Casal

Analysis reveals the commonest 2,000 words in Spanish and here they
are in frequency order, with meanings, and dual dictionary.

ARABIC KEY WORDS
David Quitregard

A hundred easy-to-master units of 20 words in Western script for the
fastest possible acquisition of the basic Arabic vocabulary.

RETHINKING ROMAN HISTORY
Jerry Toner

Is the study of Roman history properly a part of the traditional Classics
curriculum? Dr Toner argues cogently that it belongs instead in the
mainstream of history.

Find the complete Oleander list at oleanderpress.com

ISBN 0-906672-85-6

9 780906 672853 >

Made in the USA
Las Vegas, NV
21 April 2024

88976605R00085